Greenhouse Gardening

A Beginners Guide To Growing Fruit and Vegetables All Year Round

Jason Johns

Visit me at www.GardeningWithJason.com for gardening tips and advice or follow me at www.YouTube.com/OwningAnAllotment for my video diary and tips. Join me on Facebook at www.Facebook.com/OwningAnAllotment.

Find me on Twitter and Instagram as @allotmentowner and follow for updates, tips and gardening advice, plus ask me your gardening questions.

TABLE OF CONTENTS

HOW A GREENHOUSE BENEFITS YOU

Or should I title this chapter "How to Justify a Greenhouse to Your Other Half"!

A greenhouse can be a significant investment though you can find used greenhouses cheap or even free if you are willing to dismantle them and replace a few panes.

With a greenhouse, you are creating a micro-environment in which you have control over the climate. This has a whole host of benefits, which you will discover as you read this section.

Greenhouses typically have a wooden or aluminum frame and usually glass or toughened plastic panes. There are a lot of options with the materials, and some of the decisions relating to these will depend on your location and intended use of your greenhouse. But more on those later in the book.

For now, though, let's talk about how a greenhouse benefits you, which always helps in justifying the expense and time to assemble it!

Longer Growing Seasons
For those of us that live further north of the equator growing seasons never seem long enough. Even a distance of 40 miles further north can significantly alter the length of the growing season enough that you can't grow your favorite plants (trust me in that, it's devastating to realize that some plants are now a struggle to grow).

Plants grown in a greenhouse enjoy a much warmer environment, which means you can lengthen your growing time by a month or more on either end of the season. With a heater, you can lengthen it even further!

Greenhouses trap the sun's radiation, which means it gets hot in a greenhouse, allowing you to grow plants that you would otherwise be unable to grow outside. For me, it means I can not only grow tomatoes but have a long enough growing season for them to ripen and taste delicious!

Protection from the Elements
The climate is very changeable, and you can experience a heatwave and hail within the same week! This variation in weather can cause a lot of problems with your plants and stunt their growth. Squashes, in particular, are

1

susceptible to poor growth and will not produce female flowers if the weather is too cool.

When you grow in a greenhouse, you protect your plants from this variation in weather as well as damage from late frosts and high winds. It also protects your plants from torrential rain and getting too waterlogged.

It gives your plants a fighting chance, even if you only start them off in the greenhouse before moving them to a permanent site in the soil elsewhere on your vegetable plot.

With a greenhouse, you can be smug that your plants are safe while other gardeners are worrying about the damage from extreme weather.

Saving On Grocery Expenses

Yes, you can save money on your grocery bill by growing fruits and vegetables that are expensive in the stores. Being able to grow earlier and later in the year will mean you can get more produce out of the growing season.

In most cases, a greenhouse owner will make back the cost of the greenhouse in grocery savings within two or even three years of purchase!

Consistent Growing Environment

A lot of plants hate an inconsistent growing environment. When it is hot one day, cold the next then dry for a week before flooding, your plants quite naturally get upset and don't grow well.

The advantage of a greenhouse is your plants are insulated from climatic variations, and so they grow much better, maturing faster and often producing a far better crop. This helps you because your planning is no longer going to be ruined by the weather.

Plant Protection

Most vegetable plants are relatively weak when compared to weeds. Just look at how quickly weeds will grow compared to your precious vegetables. Your plants grow much stronger and faster because they do not have to compete with weeds for resources.

A greenhouse will protect your plants not only from the climate but also from seasonal pests such as locusts or Japanese beetles and to a degree from wind-borne diseases.

Optimal Growing Environment

As a gardener, you will know that a lot of vegetable plants prefer a warm, humid environment to grow. Tomatoes in particular like heat to ripen and without the right temperature will not turn red.

In a greenhouse, you can give your plants the optimal growing environment which will help them to produce a great crop for you.

Season Free Gardening

Don't you hate it when you suddenly think about planting something and realize that you can't because it is the wrong season? Or maybe you see the season drawing to a close, and your vegetables aren't quite ripe yet?

With a greenhouse, you have control over the climate, and so with the right heater, fan, and ventilation you can start your seasonal plants early or extend your growing season so your vegetables can ripen fully.

All Weather Gardening

Before I got a greenhouse, I would either get wet if it was raining or not tend to my vegetable plot. With a greenhouse, I can potter around and do something even when it is raining, which is rather pleasant.

It's a big benefit to being able to do this as being able to continue to do some work even in inclement weather is a real boon.

Multi-purpose Gardening

The lovely thing about a greenhouse is you are not just limited to growing tomatoes; you can grow anything you want!

I've seen people growing herbs, cactus plants and even bonsai trees in their greenhouse! In fact, I've just moved my cacti to my greenhouse as they are too big for the house!

The mix of plants you grow doesn't matter because they are grown in pots rather than directly in the soil. This means you can grow just about anything and mix both indoor and outdoor plants without any problems!

As you can see, there are a whole host of benefits to owning a greenhouse. With all the advantages and benefits it is a must have for any gardener and will help you to grow more plants, get better crops and get more from your vegetable plot!

PLANNING YOUR GREENHOUSE

There are a lot of considerations to be made before you buy a greenhouse. Obviously, there is budget, but other factors may well influence your budget. If you live in a particularly cold area, then double glazing and heating are important, but in a hotter area, the primary considerations would be air flow and ventilation.

What Size to Buy

Bigger is not always best, but many people aspire to a large greenhouse. What size to buy will depend on the space you have available plus what you are planning to grow. Of course, no matter what size you buy when you start to use it you will run out of space and wish you'd bought a bigger one! If you are buying a second-hand greenhouse or picking one up for free, then you have less choice in size and will usually make do with whatever comes up.

The most common size is 8' x 6' though you can get slightly smaller ones and very much larger ones. This is a good starter size, but you need to be aware that your space is limited and you will struggle to fit a lot in. However, it is a great size for starting off seeds and growing a few tomatoes or chili plants.

Check any local planning or zoning regulations before you buy a greenhouse. If you are on an allotment, then check their rules too. The last thing you want is to put up your new greenhouse only to find you have breached a rule and then have to take it down. On allotments, you often need written permission for a greenhouse and to position it in a certain way. As to HOA's, their rules are anyone's guess so check and be certain.

I would recommend visiting a shop that sells greenhouses and walking into a few different sizes. This will help you to visualize the space better and work out which one is best for you. Just remember to avoid the sales person's charm, or you may end up with a very expensive greenhouse!

When looking for a greenhouse, you need to consider how easy it is for you to maintain and use the greenhouse. If your greenhouse takes a lot of time to maintain each year, then it means less time doing other jobs.

That's the greenhouse I inherited which, as you can see, is a marvel of British engineering. Quite how it is still standing is beyond me as I understand it is well over 20 years old, but it shows what can be made with a bit of creativity!

Positioning Your Greenhouse

 Where you will put your greenhouse can influence the size, as well as other factors. Obviously, you need to position it, so it gets good sun throughout the day. Avoid north facing slopes as the amount of light will not be sufficient. Do not build your greenhouse at the bottom of a slope as it is likely to be the location of a frost pocket, meaning cold air will gather around your greenhouse. This makes your greenhouse colder, requiring more heating and reducing the benefits you get from your greenhouse.

Though if you have no choice but to site your greenhouse facing north that is still better than not having a greenhouse at all!

Depending on your preference you may choose to align your greenhouse in one of two ways.

Firstly, you can align it so the sun tracks down one side of the greenhouse. The advantage of this is that one side gets lots of sun and the other gets less allowing you to grow plants that require less sun or need a bit of shade on the side of the greenhouse furthest from the sun.

Alternatively, you can align your greenhouse, so the sun shines on one of the small ends so the whole greenhouse gets sun throughout the day.

Which you choose is up to you, and it may be that the locations available to you in your vegetable plot influences the alignment.

As an 8' x 6' greenhouse is virtually square, the alignment to the sun is not so important. For larger greenhouses, it does become more important to ensure you maximize the sun for your plants.

Something else to consider is the direction of the prevailing wind in your area. Typically, you will position the door away from the wind. This helps secure your greenhouse and make it a little less susceptible to wind damage. We will talk more about protecting your greenhouse from wind damage later in this book.

You want to position your greenhouse where it is not under trees. Should the trees lose branches, then it will damage or even destroy your greenhouse.

Ideally, you want your greenhouse located in a sheltered spot where it is not going to be subjected to high winds. This may not always be possible, but if you can do this, then it will help prevent damage in the future.

If you are planning on using an irrigation system or installing electricity, then your choice of site needs to take this into consideration. It needs to be somewhere that you can supply these services to without too much work or expense. If not, then you are stuck watering by hand and using paraffin or solar heaters like most gardeners!

Choosing the Best Floor

All of these decisions need making before you buy your greenhouse and this is probably one of the most controversial!

Which floor you choose will depend a lot on what you are planning on growing in your greenhouse and your environment.

Your choices are:

- No floor, just use the soil
- Concrete path down the middle, soil to either side
- Concrete path down the middle, weed membrane on either side
- Complete concrete floor

They all have their pros and cons, but it is a personal decision based on your site, budget, and available resources.

The picture is the inside of my inherited greenhouse. It contains a central paved path with weed membrane on either side on it laid on the soil.

The problem with this is that the weed membrane does not extend outside of the greenhouse, meaning the hard to reach edges become infested with weeds. This is okay on the left-hand side but the right-hand side has staging in place so is extremely hard to weed.

The lesson has been learned, and on my next greenhouse, the inside will be much more weed proof! But back to choosing the best floor for your greenhouse.

The first option is by far the easiest because you don't need to do anything. The downside of this is the weeds will love the heat in the greenhouse and will thrive. You will have a lot of weeding to do, and this can be very awkward to do when the plants are fully grown.

Some people do grow direct into the soil using bottomless pots. Just be aware that although this option is cheap, you will be battling weeds inside your greenhouse as well as outside. You also run the risk of introducing soil born pests and diseases if you do not change the top soil in your greenhouse every year or two.

Having a paved path down the middle of your greenhouse is great as it helps with access and isn't too expensive. You can leave the soil bare on either side or cover with a weed membrane.

This method works well, as when you put staging in your greenhouse, it becomes very hard to weed underneath it.

Putting weed membrane down will be effective in keeping the weeds away providing you use a decent quality membrane. Expect to replace it every 2 to 5 years, depending on what you use as it will perish and eventually allow weeds through.

The final option is by far the best but is also the most expensive as you have to buy paving slabs for the whole greenhouse or poured concrete. With a larger greenhouse this can soon become expensive. It is also more work as you have to lay sand and hardcore as well as level the paving.

The advantage of this method is that it is a low maintenance solution. When done properly with weed membrane under the sand, you should get years of a weed free greenhouse.

As everything will be in pots, you can also move your plants around so you can reposition them as necessary to get them more or less sun as required.

Glass vs. Polycarbonate Panes

Again this is a personal preference, and both types of panel have their good and bad points.

Glass is the more expensive solution, and the most fragile, panes can get broken by accident or vandals and need replacing.

However, glass technology is quite advanced, and you can get some great thermally insulated glass which is ideal for colder areas or heated greenhouses.

Most greenhouses use horticultural glass which typically comes in 2' square panes so you can end up with overlapping panes. The disadvantage of this type of glass is that it breaks easily into very jagged and sharp pieces. Because of the size, the panes come in you overlap them, and over time this can become dirty and grow algae, which looks unsightly.

You can buy specially toughened glass for your greenhouse, meaning it isn't going to shatter from a simple touch. It is still breakable, but it will survive an impact from a football though a more solid ball will break it. Just be careful of the edges of toughened glass as that is its weak point. When handling this make sure you never let the edges touch a rough surface.

Plastic or polycarbonate panes are much cheaper to buy and for most applications just as good as glass. The big advantage is that they are a lot

 harder break which is important if you have kids as accidents do happen.

Because the polycarbonate panes are much lighter than glass, they are also more susceptible to wind damage. In high winds, they can flex and pop out of the frame!

Glass is much heavier and gives your greenhouse a more rigid structure, something that is lacking with the polycarbonate panes.

Many polycarbonate panes are slightly opaque, meaning you cannot see in or out clearly. This may not bother you, but some people don't like it, and it can reduce the amount of sunlight your plants get.

You should also be aware that most polycarbonate panes are twin walled, meaning there are two sheets of plastic with an air gap in the middle. Over time water seeps into this gap and algae forms, which you cannot remove. This has an impact on how much light gets into your greenhouse and also looks untidy. Surprisingly, polycarbonate can cost even more than toughened glass!

Both are easy to get your hands on, being available in many glaziers. My personal preference is the plastic panes purely from the point of view that they are harder to break and less likely to smash if people throw stones at it. However, if I were to heat my greenhouse, then I would look at glass panels for better insulation and heat retention.

Half Brick Greenhouses

This type of greenhouse has several layers of bricks before the greenhouse itself starts. These are not so common these days but are still an option.

Because of the weight, you will need a more significant foundation for your greenhouse. You need to dig down about 18 inches and lay a concrete foundation which will then support the weight of the bricks and the greenhouse itself.

Also known as dwarf wall greenhouses, these harken back to Victorian times when glass was more expensive and brick cheaper. Today, though, brick is more expensive, but the greenhouse does look great and there are some advantages!

The Victorians were masters of engineering and ingenuity, and these dwarf wall greenhouses had a very specific purpose.

The brick heats up slower during the day than the glass which means it helps to keep the greenhouse cool. However, at night the bricks retain the heat and cools more slowly than the glass which keeps the greenhouse warm.

Another advantage is that brick doesn't break. Typically, it will be the lower panes that break as you mow or strim around the greenhouse and kick up stones.

Of course, these half brick greenhouses also look great and are a fine addition to any garden.

Wood vs. Aluminum Frames

Wooden frames look great on a greenhouse, but they are more expensive and will require regular maintenance. You will need to treat the wood every year to prevent it from rotting and keep it looking great. Eventually, though the wood will need replacing and it can be difficult and time-consuming to replace single pieces of wood.

Wooden framed greenhouses look great and when looked after will last for many years. Because of their weight and natural strength, they are less susceptible to wind damage. So if you live in an area with high winds, then it may be worth investing in a wooden frame to prevent damage to your greenhouse.

When you order a wooden frame greenhouse, it will usually come in sections that you put together. For the smaller size greenhouses, it will come as two side panels, two end panels, and two roof panels.

All you need to do is bolt it all together, though you will need help due to the weight of the wood and size of the panels.

Larger greenhouses will come with more panels. You will need to ensure you have suitable access to your greenhouse site so you can get the panels to the right place.

Aluminum frames are much cheaper to buy and will usually come flat packed, so you have to assemble it yourself. They will also usually fit in your car so you can take them home then and there rather than wait for delivery.

This does mean you can do a lot of it by yourself as it is much lighter than wood, but it is also more likely to twist. With an aluminum greenhouse, you need to ensure that the greenhouse is square and level, which can take time.

Although much more affordable than wood, aluminum is a lot lighter. This means you need to take extra care to secure it to the ground to prevent wind damage. High winds will tear an aluminum greenhouse to pieces, twisting the frame and shattering the glass. When properly secured though it can survive all but the most severe storms.

Some greenhouses come with powder coated frames which gives them a nice color. A powder coated frame will last a good ten years without any treatment and can last 15 to 25 years without any need to paint, which surely is good news for us all!

Powder coating is a chemical process which coats the aluminum frame with colored powder. This is baked on. The range of colors available is good though you will need to get your greenhouse from a supplier that offers this service. You can expect to pay a premium price for this coating though.

Which you choose is up to you, but most of us will go for aluminum frames purely from an affordability point of view.

Greenhouses vs. Polytunnels

In many ways, a polytunnel is very similar to a greenhouse in that it insulates your plants from the weather and helps them thrive.

Polytunnels are typically made from plastic or aluminum pipes and covered with a strong plastic sheeting.

These are much cheaper than greenhouses, but they aren't quite the same. We will discuss polytunnels in the Hoop House section later in the book.

A polytunnel is much weaker than a greenhouse and more likely to be damaged in high winds. It also does not provide the same level of insulation as a greenhouse. It is still excellent for growing plants and keeping them warm, but in the colder months, it will be harder to heat and keep warm.

A lot of serious growers will start their plants off in a greenhouse before moving them into a polytunnel to complete their growing season. Frost tender plants are then often moved back into the greenhouse in winter for that extra protection from the weather.

A polytunnel is a good starter for growing with many similar considerations to a greenhouse. Remember to buy the strongest you can afford and secure it against the wind fully.

Making A Foundation For Your Greenhouse

When you are building a greenhouse, the first step is to build a foundation. This needs to be done properly for you to have a solid greenhouse that will stand the test of time.

Whatever you decide to make your foundation out of, it needs to be both level and square. It needs to be big enough for the outside dimensions of the greenhouse to ensure it fits properly and can be secured.

You can buy pre-made greenhouse bases, and these are worth considering, but just be aware that these still need a flat and level surface to be installed on and will still need a foundation beneath them.

When building your greenhouse base, you can either make it out of poured concrete, or you can use sand and paving stones. Both are suitable and do the job well, though the latter has the advantage of being moveable in the future if necessary.

Ensure that not only are the edges of your base square but also that the diagonal measurements between the corners are also identical.

Under the base, you will need the foundation which is what supports the weight of the greenhouse, which it is secured to and prevents damage in windy weather.

If you live in an area where the ground freezes then your greenhouse foundation needs to be below the frost line. This is to prevent damage to your structure from the ground heaving as it freezes and melts. Your local Building Permit Agency will be able to tell you where the frost line is in your area. In warmer areas, this is only going to be a couple of inches at most, but in the colder, northern areas it can be as much as a few feet.

One good way of insulating your foundation and protecting it is to use 1" foam insulation. Put this down to your frost line to reduce heat loss through the soil, which has the benefit of reducing your heating costs.

The foundation is essential because this is what you are securing your greenhouse too. It will prevent weather damage and warping in hot or cold weather. If you do not secure your greenhouse properly, then don't expect it to last the growing season. If the greenhouse starts to warp, then you can find your panes shatter or crack and become very hard to re-fit. You can also find doors and windows become stiff and very difficult to use too.

If you have bought a new greenhouse, then any warranty will not cover damage due to not having a proper greenhouse base.

Your greenhouse is built on this foundation and base, which will ensure it is easier to erect and that it will last.

There are some different choices for the foundation.

Compacted Soil

If you compact the soil enough, then you can build your greenhouse directly on the ground, particularly if you live in an area where the ground doesn't freeze too badly.

A lot of greenhouses will come with an optional metal plinth which has spikes in each corner. These can be cemented into the ground to prevent the base from moving.

You will still need to level the ground though, so dig out your spirit level. It is best to use a roller or other mechanical device to compact the soil to ensure it is stable. Do not build your base out of gravel or hardcore because these are just not stable enough.

The advantage of using the soil as your foundation is that it is very cost effective. You can also use the existing ground for growing your plants in plus drainage is a lot better.

The downside of soil is that it will allow pests into your greenhouse. You will find this particularly bad in winter as pests flock to your greenhouse for the warmth.

However, for a greenhouse bigger than about 8' x 10' this is not suitable because of the weight of the frame. When using the ground as your foundation, you are risking damage to your greenhouse if the ground moves through subsidence or isn't compacted properly.

You will need a metal greenhouse base to build your greenhouse on and secure that to the ground. It is also quite hard to get the soil level plus you will have to deal with weeds growing up from the soil too.

The soil does have a nasty habit of clogging up your door runners, so you will have to brush that out regularly.

Perimeter Bases

This is a slightly cheaper option where you use either bricks, breeze blocks or thin paving or edging slabs to create a foundation directly under the greenhouse frame. You can use concrete if you prefer.

The foundation is built along where the frame will run, leaving the soil in the middle of the greenhouse untouched.

While you can build the foundation directly on the soil, most people will cut out a trench and place the foundation in the trench. The advantage of this latter approach is that it is easier to level.

This offers all the benefits of a fully slabbed base but without the associated cost as you are using fewer materials.

You have a lot of options for growing either direct in the soil, making a central pathway or using a weed membrane.

It is very easy to prepare and can be quite decorative. However, you have to be very accurate with your measurements because there isn't a lot of room for error.

Slabs or Paving

This is a great way to build a greenhouse foundation because it keeps out the weeds and pests while giving you a good, clean growing environment.

This method involves building a base the size of your greenhouse out of paving slabs and then fixing your greenhouse to it. This type of base will last for many years and is very low maintenance.

You can screw your greenhouse to the base to provide stability in windy conditions, preventing any damage. It also provides good drainage when compared to an all concrete base.

In the winter months, a soil floor can get damp and encourage mold to grow. A paved floor helps to keep the greenhouse both warmer and drier in the cooler months.

Providing you bed down the slabs properly with an inch or two of sand underneath them they are surprisingly easy to get level and will not warp or move over time.

However, this is more expensive to build and requires more work. You will not be able to grow direct in the soil and will have to use containers and grow bags, which most people consider a necessity in a greenhouse.

Concrete Base

This is where you mark out where your greenhouse will be and dig down a few inches before pouring concrete in to form the base.

For larger greenhouses, this has its advantages, but it can be expensive and does require specialist tools such as a concrete mixer.

This is a very durable base, and you can fit expansion bolts to secure larger structures. You may have an issue with standing water so may want to consider putting drainage holes in to prevent standing water.

Greenhouse Floor

Drainage is very important in a greenhouse as if the environment is too damp then it will encourage mold, and your plants will rot.

Although you can use compacted soil, it comes with a whole host of potential problems that will make growing in a greenhouse more difficult, increasing your workload over the year. In most cases, the disadvantages of compacted soil far outweigh the advantages.

Before you lay any floor, the first thing to do is put down a good quality weed membrane. Don't skimp here and buy the cheap fabric as that will let the weeds through. Spend the extra money to buy a good quality woven plastic membrane to prevent weeds from getting into your greenhouse.

Don't be tempted to use a normal plastic liner because these are not water permeable. Water will pool on top of the plastic liner and flood your greenhouse. Although you can make holes in the plastic liner to let water through, doing so will let the weeds come up into the greenhouse.

14

If you are laying paving slabs, then you need to put sand underneath them which will help with drainage. With mortared slabs or a concrete floor, you will need to install some drainage holes to allow water to drain away. Just ensure that your drainage holes do not allow weeds to get in.

Some people will use pea sized gravel as their greenhouse floor which does work and makes for a good floor. You do need to use a good quality weed membrane underneath it. Soil tends to build up in gravel over time as it comes in through the door or is dropped out of containers. This will encourage weeds to grow in it and you end up having to weed it. Most people will replace the gravel every few years to prevent this from becoming too much of a problem.

Start your paving slab floor by laying a good quality membrane underneath it. Cover this with about 2" of finely crushed rock. Then build a frame of treated wood which follows the edge of your greenhouse and marks out any walkways. Then spread sand to about 1" deep, pressing it down firmly. Lay your pavers, leaving about ½" between each one. Then fill the gaps with sand, using a brush to clear sand off the slabs.

A concrete floor is laid with a little bit more consideration. You have to work out how you are going to drain the floor before you start to lay it. In most cases, the floor will have plastic tubes going down into the soil which excess water drains into. Under each tube will be a drain sump, i.e. a large amount of gravel to ensure water soaks away quickly and doesn't back up the tube to flood the greenhouse.

Alternatively, you can make the floor slightly slanted, so water drains off to one side, and there you place your drain sump.

The advantage of a concrete floor is that it is easy to clean and will retain heat though it is more time consuming and costly to install.

Before pouring your concrete floor, you will dig down a couple of inches. You need to fill the base with about 2" of gravel and tamp it down to ensure it is well packed.

On top of this, the concrete is poured to between an inch or two deep, depending on your needs. Once the base has dried, build a 2x4" wood sill on which you anchor your greenhouse.

Place ½" x 9" anchor bolts into the concrete with about 1½" above the surface. Countersink the nuts into the wood sill and the greenhouse attached to this. Set the bolts within a foot of each corner with additional bolts every 3 to 4 feet.

This is a very important part of constructing a greenhouse and must be done properly to avoid problems and extra expense in the future. Do this well and it will give you years of service!

BUYING A USED GREENHOUSE

For many people buying a new greenhouse is just too expensive. They aren't cheap, and the cost means many people do not buy one.

A good option is to buy a used greenhouse either through eBay, Freecycle, Gumtree or local ads. Often these are a fraction of the price of a new greenhouse, and you can even find greenhouses for free! Some people, when they move into a new home, find a greenhouse they don't want and will offer it for free to someone who is willing to come and take it away.

When buying a used greenhouse, you will be expected in many cases to disassemble the greenhouse yourself. Take lots of pictures of the greenhouse before you take it apart as it will help you to put it back together again. Make notes on any non-standard panes and where they belong. Plenty of pictures from all angles is the easiest way to do this.

Taking a greenhouse down and reassembling it will be a two-person job, so you need to find yourself a helper to make the job easier.

You will need some tools to take down the greenhouse including a wide selection of spanners, both open and closed ended. You will also need a variety of screwdrivers, both flat and cross-head, and also large ones. A ratchet spanner will help you a lot and make things easier. A good pair of pliers can also help with the more stubborn bolts.

I would also recommend a can of WD-40 to help ease rusted bolts as well as a junior hacksaw for those exceptionally stubborn bolts.

You should wear gloves, particularly while moving the glass otherwise you will end up with plenty of cuts on your hands.

Ideally, you will want to disassemble the greenhouse on a dry day because doing it in the rain is unpleasant (trust me on this) and much harder as everything becomes slippery.

It is worthwhile labeling parts as you take them apart as it will help you a lot when putting it back together. If you can get a van, then you don't have to take the greenhouse down completely. You can just break it into the front, rear and side panels and the two halves of the roof and fit them in the van. It will save you a lot of work if you can do it this way!

Most used greenhouses will be on the smaller side, usually 8x6' or thereabouts. If you want a larger greenhouse, then just get two smaller greenhouses and join them together!

As with any greenhouse, the first thing you need to do is build a base following instructions from previous chapters. Just make sure that the base is square (measure the diagonals) and level (use a spirit level that is at least 3 feet long).

Before you dive headlong into assembling your greenhouse you need to sort out all the bits and pieces. Make sure you have enough nuts and bolts and that those you have are usable. Sometimes they can be rusted or the thread stripped, so you will want to have enough to hand. The last thing you want is to be halfway through when you discover you are missing vital parts. Buy these from most home improvement stores or online.

Also, make sure you have plenty of glass clips as these often go missing or get broken when taking a greenhouse to pieces.

Make sure all the glass pieces are present, and none are broken. You cannot assemble your greenhouse without all the panes as that will make it extremely susceptible to wind damage.

Check the weather forecast before you start building your greenhouse as doing it in the rain is no fun and doing it in high winds is positively dangerous!

Sort the struts out, group them together into each of the sides and the roof. This allows you to check you have all the pieces and then assemble each side before you put it all together.

Once the frame is assembled, you need to start putting the glass in place.

This is best done from the top down because you can get around the greenhouse better without glass in the frame beneath you. This is when you realize that your glazing clips are broken, twisted or even missing, so buy a bag or two before you start! Remember that glass doesn't bend, so you need to be careful putting it in. An 8x6' greenhouse can end up using up to 200 of these clips!

It is also worthwhile buying some extra rubber seals that the glass fits into. Invariably when taking a greenhouse to pieces, these will break or get lost.

Buy all the spare parts you need before you start reassembling the greenhouse. It will make your life much easier.

Just remember to be careful when reassembling your greenhouse. The glass can and will break so transport it with care. It isn't a race so just take your time and make sure you have someone to help you!

Air Flow, Cooling & Humidity

Air flow is very important for healthy plant growth in a greenhouse, particularly in the heat of summer as temperatures (hopefully) soar. The air needs to keep moving which will prevent heat building up and damaging your plants.

Most greenhouses will come with vents and/or windows to help with the movement of air. A good quality greenhouse will have louver vents at ground level which draw in cold air (which is heavier than hot air) and then vents at the top which allows hot air to rise out of the greenhouse. This creates a very natural movement of air which your plants appreciate.

You are looking for a greenhouse with windows and vents that account for around a third of the entire roof area. They do not all need to be at roof level and, ideally, you will want vents at different levels.

If your greenhouse isn't suitably ventilated, then you are going to encourage all sorts of diseases such as fungal problems, powdery mildew, and botrytis. Worse still a greenhouse that is too hot will end up killing some of your plants.

You can leave the door open in the summer, but this can be a security problem depending on where your greenhouse is located.

The other disadvantage of leaving a door open is that pets, particularly cats, will decide to investigate your greenhouse. Dogs, cats, and chickens will cause havoc in your greenhouse from eating plants and fruits to sitting on plants. If you do have pets and want to leave the door open, then a wire panel will keep out most animals except cats.

Window or door screens can be used to keep out unwanted visitors, but the downside of these is that they can also keep out vital pollinating insects!

Mice and other rodents can find their way into your greenhouse through open windows or doors so it can be worth installing an ultrasonic device to keep them out. Of course, cats are excellent rodent deterrents but cause their own unique brand of chaos!

Shade Cloth and Paint

This is one of the simplest ways for you to provide shade for your plants.

Shade paint is applied to the outside of your glass, and it diffuses the sun and keeps some of the heat out. Modern shade paints are very clever and will react to the sunlight. When it is raining then the shade paint remains clear, but as the sun comes out, the paint turns white, reflects the sunlight.

Shade fabric is another way to cool your greenhouse, and this is put on the outside of your greenhouse to prevent the sunlight getting to your plants. It is best installed on the outside of your greenhouse, but you can put it inside, though it will not be as effective. When it is outside, it stops the sun's rays penetrating your greenhouse but when on the inside the sunlight is already in the greenhouse and generating heat.

Shading alone though is not going to protect your plants from heat damage. Combine this with good ventilation and humidity control to provide your plants with the best possible growing environment.

Shade cloth is a lightweight polyethylene knitted fabric available in densities from 30% to 90% to keep out less or more of the sun's rays. It is not only suitable for greenhouses but is used in cold frames and other applications. It is mildew and rot resistant, water permeable and does not become brittle over time.

It provides great ventilation and diffuses the light, keeping your greenhouse cooler. It can help reduce the need to run fans in the summer and is quick to install and remove.

A reflective shade is good because instead of absorbing the sun's rays it reflects it. This is better if you can get hold of it because it will be more efficient at keeping the greenhouse cool. The reflective shade cloth is more expensive than normal shade cloth, but it is worth the money for the additional benefits.

For most applications, you will want a shade cloth that is 50% or 60% density, but in hotter climates or with light sensitive plants higher densities such as 70% to 80% will be necessary. A lot of people use higher density shade cloth on the roof and a lower density cloth on the walls.

Shade cloth is typically sold by the foot or meter, depending on where you are located, though you can find it sold in pre-made sizes. These are usually hemmed and include grommets for attaching the cloth to the greenhouse.

A shade cloth with a density of 70% allows 30% of light to pass through it. For most vegetables, in that majority of climates, a shade cloth of 30% to 50% will be sufficient. If you are shading people, then you will want to go up to a density of 80% or 90%.

Air Flow

Keeping the air moving in your greenhouse during summer can be difficult, particularly in larger greenhouses. Many of the larger electrical greenhouse heaters will double up as air blowers in the summer just by using the fan without the heating element being turned on.

However, using a fan is down to whether or not you have electricity in your greenhouse, which not all of us will have. Although you can use solar energy to run your fan, you will find that it is hard to generate enough energy to keep it going all day.

Automatic Vents

These are an absolute godsend for any gardener and will help keep your plants alive and stop you having to get up early to open vents! Automatic vents will open the windows as the temperature rises. This is usually by a cylinder of wax which expands in the heat, opening the window and then contracts as the temperature cools which closes the window. These do have a finite lifetime, lasting a few years but are easily replaced.

One technique which can help keep your greenhouse cool is to damp down the paths and the floor. As the water evaporates, it will help keep the greenhouse cool.

Remember too that some plants can be moved outside in the heat of the summer which will free up space in your greenhouse and help airflow.

An alternative to the wax openers is a solar powered automatic opener. These work in a similar manner, opening the vents as the temperatures increase. These are a little bit more expensive than the mechanical auto-openers though work well.

Choosing an Exhaust Fan

For larger greenhouses, you will want an exhaust fan. This is overkill for a smaller greenhouse, but anyone choosing a larger structure will benefit from installing one.

Your exhaust fan needs to be able to change the air in your greenhouse in between 60 and 90 seconds. Fans are rated by cubic feet per minute (CFM), for which you will need to calculate the volume of your greenhouse which is done simply by multiplying the length by the width by the average height.

To measure the average height, measure straight down to the floor from halfway up a roof rafter. It doesn't have to be precise as a few inches either way isn't going to make a significant difference.

To determine the cubic feet per minute rating, you need you simply multiply the volume by 0.75. Then you will need to find a fan that is near to or greater than this value.

Be careful and double check your calculations as a fan that is too small

21

will not provide you with enough cooling. Together with a fan, shading cloth or paint and damping down it will help ensure the greenhouse is kept cool and your plants thrive.

As an example, if your greenhouse is 8' by 10' with an average height of 7' this will give you a calculation of 8x10x7 which is 560 cubic feet.

So, therefore, you will need a fan that is rated at least 560 CFM for sufficient cooling.

You will also need to calculate the shutter size. Do this by dividing your fan CFM by 250 which gives a shutter size in square feet.

For greenhouses over 100 square feet or wider than 8 feet two shutters are required, so you will need to divide this figure by two to get the size for each shutter.

The fan needs to be positioned as high as possible, typically at the end opposite to the door. The motor needs to be on the inside of the greenhouse, and the fan can be mounted either on the inside or outside as convenient for you.

The shutters are installed at the opposite end to the exhaust fan. For those without a motor, they are installed with the vanes opening into your greenhouse. Motorized shutters are installed with the motor on the inside of the greenhouse and the vanes opening outwards.

Ventilating your greenhouse is extremely important and something many growers overlook. Plants need air flow to stay healthy. Poor airflow is a major contributing factor to fungal infections which plants such as cucumber and tomatoes are particularly susceptible too.

Ensuring your plants are not too crowded will also help a lot with air flow and preventing fungal infections.

Although your greenhouse may be too small for a fan or you may not have any electricity, at the very least you need windows though louver vents will help a lot. Making sure there is adequate ventilation in your greenhouse is vital so don't skip this step when setting up your greenhouse!

GREENHOUSE IRRIGATION SYSTEMS

One of the main issues you will face with a greenhouse is keeping your plants watered. In hot weather, they can dry out very quickly, and this can cause problems such as leaf, flower or fruit drop which you obviously want to avoid.

If your greenhouse is in your garden then it is easy enough to pop down and water it, but if it is at an allotment or you are on holiday then watering becomes much trickier, putting your harvest at risk.

In the hottest weather, and more so in hotter climates, you will need to water your plants two or three times a day to keep them healthy no matter how good your cooling system is!

Although you can hand water the plants in your greenhouse, this can soon get boring and difficult to keep up. The best and most efficient way to water your plants is to invest in a greenhouse irrigation system. Which you choose will depend on the size of your greenhouse, what you are growing and whether or not you have electricity and water to hand.

If you are planning to irrigate your greenhouse, then the need to be sited near to water and/or electricity can heavily influence your choice of location.

There are a lot of different irrigation systems on the market with widely varying prices, so you do need to spend some time considering your requirements before rushing out to buy one.

Some plants require more water than others, so depending on what you are growing you may want to get an automatic irrigation system that can deliver differing quantities of water to different plants.

You also want a system that can grow with you as you put more plants in your greenhouse. At certain times within the season you will have more plants in your greenhouse than at others, so your irrigation system needs to be able to support this extra demand.

You do need to be careful because any irrigation system that is introducing too much water to your greenhouse could end up making it too damp, which will encourage the growth of diseases. This is one reason why you need to have your drainage and ventilation right to prevent damage to your greenhouse ecosystem.

You typically have two choices about how to deliver water to your plants, either through spray heads or a drip system. The former will spray water over everything in your greenhouse. The downside of this is that it can encourage powdery mildew on certain plants, but the spray can help damp down your greenhouse. It can also be a bit hit and miss as to how much ends up in the soil of your plants. If you are growing in containers, then a spray system may not deliver water precisely enough.

Drip systems though will deliver water precisely to containers and give each container exactly the right amount of water, so no plant goes thirsty!

The downside of most irrigation systems is that they require electricity, which can be difficult, expensive or even impossible for some greenhouse owners to install. You can purchase solar powered irrigation systems which will do the job, but they can struggle on duller days.

The water will come into the greenhouse with piping and correctly locating this is important. Hanging it from the ceiling and running it along the walls helps keep it out of the way and stops it getting damaged. Running the piping along the floor is a recipe for disaster as you are bound to end up putting a container on it and damaging it!

You will need a water supply and ideally mains water, but you can run some irrigation systems from water butts. You will have to check regularly that the water butt has enough water in it, but it is still much easier than manually watering your plants!

Overhead Misters

If you grow mostly or all one type of plant, then an overhead watering method is a great choice because you can water all your plants evenly and easily. For larger greenhouses, this is a great system because it will water a large area quickly.

The downside of this type of system is that it is quite wasteful of water because the water goes everywhere in the greenhouse, not just into the containers where your plants are.

Your plants end up getting a lot of water on their leaves. If they are over-crowded or ventilation is poor, then this can cause problems such as powdery mildew and make your plants more susceptible to disease.

Mat Irrigation

You can buy capillary matting which works as an irrigation system for your plants. This is a special mat that is designed to draw up water which is then absorbed by your plants through moisture wicks which go into the soil of your containers.

The mat is kept moist by a drip watering system, so you do not have to run water piping throughout your greenhouse. It can just go to strategic points where it feeds the capillary matting.

This is a relatively cheap method of irrigation and is very simple to install. The big advantage is it is very efficient in its use of water, and there is little risk of overwatering your plants!

Drip Tubing

This is special tubing that you run throughout your greenhouse. It has tubes attached to it that run to the roots of each container to supply water directly to the soil. The big advantage of most drip systems is that you can control the amount of water dripped into your plants. This means that plants that need more water can get it and plants that need less don't get over-watered.

This is set to drip at a certain rate or to operate on a timer so it waters at regular intervals. It will depend on the type of system you buy as to whether it is constant or timed. Timed is by far the best as it allows greater control of the delivery of water, reducing the risks of over-watering.

This is a very water efficient method of watering your greenhouse with minimal wastage. It can also be set up to be completely automatic, which reduces the time you spend managing your greenhouse.

With some of the more advanced drip watering systems, you have sensors in the ground that monitor moisture levels and turn on the water when the soil becomes too dry.

If you are growing directly in the soil, then the type of soil will influence your drip rate. A heavy clay soil will take longer to absorb water, so it needs less water than a lighter soil because in clay it will puddle and pool, which you want to avoid.

When you are growing a variety of plants, this is by far the best irrigation method because you can control the amount of water each container receives.

Planning your drip watering system is relatively easy. You need to divide your greenhouse into an equal number of sections, and each area will hold plants with similar water requirements. Depending on the size of your greenhouse you may need multiple irrigation systems, but most are easy to expand with additional piping.

Drip irrigation piping comes in either black polyethylene (PE) or polyvinyl chloride (PVC). These are cheap, easy to handle and bendy when you need it to be.

PVC pipe is often used in supply and header lines as you can solvent bond connections and fittings. Polyethylene connections though need to be clamped. PVC pipe is also more durable, being less sensitive to temperature fluctuations and sunlight but it is more expensive to buy.

Polyethylene pipe is sensitive to high temperatures and will contract and expand. This means it can move out of position unless it is held in place.

Your main feeder piping may be 1" or 2" wide but for lateral, emitter lines ½" piping is sufficient. Each row of plants will have its own ½" line containing emitters. In smaller greenhouses, you can get away with one emitter line for every two rows when plants are spaced less than 18-20" apart.

There are some different types of emitter available. The perforated hose or porous pipe types are very common and are an emitter line with holes in it. The water then seeps out of these holes. Most will deliver water at a rate of anywhere from ½ to 3 gallons an hour. The rate of delivery is changed by adjusting the water pressure.

Alternatively, you can get emitter valves which allows you to control the drip rate for each pot.

Emitters are usually spaced between 24" and 36" along the main lateral lines.

One thing to remember is that you need to filter the water, particularly if it is coming out of a water butt. This will prevent any dirt getting into the system and clogging the emitters. This is vital as it will ensure your irrigation system works without any problems.

Some irrigation systems will allow you to install a fertilizer injector. This is useful as you can get your irrigation system to automatically feed your plants too! Depending on the system this can be set to deliver liquid fertilizer constantly or at specified intervals. This, though, is typically found in more expensive systems, and you need to be very careful in your choice of liquid feed to prevent clogging up the system.

The key with drip irrigation systems is to apply a little water frequently to maintain the soil moisture levels. This is a very water efficient system that is easy to expand and works no matter what size plants you are growing.

Most people who own a greenhouse and install an irrigation system will choose a drip watering system. They are easily available and very affordable though, as with anything, you can spend more money and get more advanced systems.

HEATING YOUR GREENHOUSE

For most people growing will end as temperatures start to drop, even though a greenhouse can extend the growing season by a few weeks.

To grow throughout the year or to keep frost tender plants alive over winter you will need to heat your greenhouse. Depending on what you are growing you may get away with just keeping the frost off, or you may need to heat the greenhouse to warmer temperatures. A heating mat may help you to germinate seeds, but plant growth is severely slowed in the colder months.

A greenhouse does help to keep your plants warmer, and it will help to keep frost from your plants. However, if temperatures plummet too far then no matter how well built your greenhouse, it will not keep out the frost.

Before you decide upon a heating solution for your greenhouse, you need to decide what you are growing. Different crops have different temperature requirements, and if you are growing plants which are frost hardy or tolerate cooler temperatures, then you do not need to heat your greenhouse as much.

Warmer weather crops such as tomatoes, chilies, and peppers are going to be extremely difficult to grow in a greenhouse in colder areas over winter as the heater simply will not be able to keep up. To heat your greenhouse enough, you would have to spend a fortune on heating which would simply not make the investment cost-effective.

A simple, eco-friendly way to keep your greenhouse warm is to dig out a trench down the middle of your greenhouse, cover it with palettes and then make compost in it. In smaller greenhouses, this isn't going to be a huge area, but it will help to raise the temperature in your greenhouse without investing in heating equipment.

Another free heating technique is to paint some barrels, buckets or sandbags black and leave them in your greenhouse. These will absorb heat during the day and radiate it back out at night. It isn't going to make more than a degree or two difference, but it could be enough to keep the frost off of your plants.

The easiest way to heat your greenhouse is with an electric heater, though this does require you to have electricity in your greenhouse. Running an extension cord out isn't safe so if you are installing electricity then get it done professionally and safely. It has to be waterproof if it is outside and there are likely rules and regulations in your country affecting how and where the cable can be run.

You need to ensure that your electric heat is stable and that it is away from flammable material. You also need to be cautious when watering your plants to ensure you do not damage your heater.

When using an electric heater, it is important that the air circulates properly. This will prevent hot spots as well as cold spots and also reduce condensation. Some heaters have fans built in but others will need additional air circulation.

As the price of propane has been increasing many greenhouse owners are turning to wood or pellet stoves. These are working out to be very cost effective even on a larger scale. You will need to check local codes and follow their requirements as well as follow common sense safety precautions. Pellet stoves are very easy to use, often come with temperature controls, and some even have blowers which will circulate the heat.

If your greenhouse is plastic, then a wood stove is not a good idea. The stove pipe gets very hot and will melt plastic. Ideally, your stove should be vented out through a masonry foundation or something similar rather than through glass.

Another alternative is to cover your greenhouse with plastic and line the inside with bubble wrap. This is a good solution in areas where the temperature doesn't drop too far in winter. However, in areas where there are months of freezing weather, this will not keep the frost out of your greenhouse.

You can buy specific insulation for your greenhouse which will help reduce heat loss and your heating bill. This is often put in place as the temperature drops and removed when spring has arrived.

There are propane, natural gas, petrol and other heaters available and these are effective. They are getting more expensive to buy, but they do a good job in a greenhouse which cannot have electricity. Many people with smaller, garden greenhouses will use a propane heater. The advantage of these heaters is you do not need to have electricity in your greenhouse, meaning your greenhouse can be sited anywhere.

Heaters are rated in British Thermal Units or BTU's. The higher the BTU, then the more heat it gives out. You can calculate the number of BTU's you need for your greenhouse using formulas found online or heater suppliers will help you. You will need to take into account a number of factors including the size of your greenhouse, how hot you want the greenhouse, the heat loss of the greenhouse and more. Getting this right means you do not waste energy heating your greenhouse or buying a heater that won't do the job.

Natural gas heaters require a gas line to be run to your greenhouse whereas propane heaters run on gas cylinders, making them the most popular heaters with home greenhouse owners.

Where to Put Your Heater

Where you locate your heater will depend on some factors such as the location of vents and shutters, where the doors are and more.

You need to be careful that where you site your heater isn't under a water leak or anything similar.

Depending on the floor in your greenhouse it may be necessary to build a plinth to mount your heater on. This will ensure the heater is level and safe.

Consider all the factors and if you are still unsure then speak to any supplier of heaters, and they will be able to advise you.

Types of Greenhouse Heaters

There are many different types of greenhouse heater on the market, and we touched on these already. Let's go into more detail now on these different heaters together with their advantages and disadvantages.

Paraffin Greenhouse Heaters

Paraffin heaters are one of the most popular ways to heat a greenhouse, being both affordable and readily available. For a home gardener with a smaller greenhouse these are ideal, but as the price of paraffin has increased in recent years, this has made these less popular.

You can buy paraffin cheaper online or in bulk, but the heaters are cheap to buy new. There is also a healthy market for used paraffin heaters, so it does make this a very affordable solution.

Paraffin heaters come in some different sizes and in most models the paraffin reservoir is large enough to last a day, or even two so are low maintenance. Being self-contained they have no requirement for electricity, and they also give off CO_2 which your plants will appreciate.

Paraffin has become less popular in recent years because of the cost of the fuel which has become harder to obtain. However, in our Internet age, it is easier now to source this fuel, though with the concerns about climate change and emissions this type of fuel is likely to wane in popularity still further.

This type of heat is always on and is manually controlled. You can end up with the heater burning when heat isn't needed and wasting fuel. There are no temperature controls on a paraffin heater as it just burns. You can often adjust the size of the flame, but there is usually no way to turn off the heat when the greenhouse reaches a set temperature.

One disadvantage of paraffin heaters is that they give off water vapor which can encourage mold if the greenhouse isn't suitably ventilated.

Electric Greenhouse Heaters

These are a great form of heating, but it does require your greenhouse to have an electricity supply. Electric heaters are controlled by a thermostat so you have greater control over the heat output and therefore over your running costs.

Because of the dangers of mixing water with electricity you have to make sure you get a heater that is designed to work in a greenhouse and that the electricity supply is safe and protected from water and damp.

Electric heaters are not for everyone because of the cost of running electric cable to a greenhouse. If you are on an allotment site, then you are very unlikely to have access to electricity. Depending on local regulations you may need to hire a professional to lay the cable and use armored cable.

The advantage of an electric fan heater is that it does circulate air around the greenhouse which avoids hot and cold spots. This also helps to reduce the risk of fungal problems from poor air circulation.

Propane Gas Heaters

Run from propane bottles these are relatively cheap to run, and propane can be refilled at many camping stores or gas stations. For a greenhouse without electricity, these are a viable solution.

You will need to ensure your greenhouse is well ventilated because propane gas heaters produce water vapor. They also produce CO_2 which your plants will appreciate.

Many propane heaters come with thermostatic controls which gives you a degree of control over your running costs.

Mains Gas Heating

This is an excellent method of heating larger greenhouses. The installation costs are high, but the running costs are reasonable.

You will need a natural gas pipe run to your greenhouse. Again this is not for everyone, and in most cases, natural gas is not going to be a cost effective form of heating your greenhouse.

This is most popular with commercial growers in large greenhouses and isn't something most home growers will install.

Greenhouse Heating Tips

Obviously, you want to keep your heating costs down during winter while keeping your plants warm and alive. Here are some of my favorite tips to effectively and efficiently heat your greenhouse.

- Bubble Wrap Is Your Friend – clip bubble wrap to the inside of your greenhouse frame to help reduce heat loss and block draughts. You can buy horticultural bubble wrap which is both toughened and UV stabilized. Remember that larger bubbles will let more light get into your greenhouse to your plants. This bubble wrap can also be used on tender outdoors plants and pots to protect them from frost.

- Don't Be Afraid of the Thermostat – if your heater has a thermostat then use it! You can set your heater only to come on when temperatures go below a certain point. You may need to experiment with the temperature a little so that the heat kicks in and heats your greenhouse before the plants get too cold.

- Choose The Right Temperature – most plants are not going to appreciate a tropical jungle temperature so if you are just preventing frost all you need to do is keep your greenhouse at 2C/36F. Some tender plants including citrus trees prefer a higher minimum temperature of 7C/45F as will many young plants. Delicate plants will require higher temperatures, depending on the plant.

- Buy A Thermometer – a good thermometer that can record maximum and minimum temperatures is going to help you a lot with your greenhouse. By knowing how low the temperature drops at night you will be able to use your heater more efficiently and save yourself some money. It also helps you understand how hot your greenhouse gets during the day, so you know whether or not you need to cool it down.

- Think About Heater Position – where you locate the heaters will influence how well your greenhouse is heated. Electric heaters are positioned away from water, and so it circulates the air around the greenhouse. With all heaters you need to be careful they don't point directly at plants and dry out the leaves.

- Heat What You Need to – heating a greenhouse can be expensive so if you only have a few delicate plants then put them in one place, surround them with a bubble wrap or Perspex curtain and then heat just that area. There is no point you spending money heating a greenhouse that is mostly empty when all you need to do is heat a small area.

- Use Horticultural Fleece – on the coldest nights a couple of layers of this will give your plants that extra bit of protection by raising their temperature a few vital degrees. Remember though to remove the fleece during the day, so the plants are well ventilated and don't overheat.

- Ventilate – heating your greenhouse increases humidity, so it is vital that you have good ventilation. This will keep your greenhouse healthy and prevent the build-up of fungal diseases.

- Water Early On – you can help reduce the humidity in your greenhouse by watering your plants earlier on in the day. Give the plants the water they need and try not to overwater or water the floor in your greenhouse unless you are damping down.
- Use Your Vents Wisely – open your greenhouse vents early in the morning on sunny days to clear condensation. Close them before the sun goes down, so you trap the warmth of the day in the greenhouse. This will help your heaters to be more efficient.
- Use a Heated Propagator – if you are germinating seeds in your greenhouse you do not need to heat the entire greenhouse unless you are starting off a lot of seeds. A heated propagation mat will help keep your seeds and seedlings warm without the expense of heating the whole greenhouse.

Depending on what you are growing and how much you want to extend your growing season you may want to heat your greenhouse. For many people though the cost is excessive and it isn't practical to do so. A small paraffin or propane heater though can be enough to keep the frost out of your greenhouse, extending the growing season enough so your tomatoes, peppers, and chilies have time to ripen fully!

THE GROUND VS CONTAINERS

You have two options when it comes to growing plants in your greenhouse. You can grow them directly in the ground, or you can grow them in containers.

Both methods have their advantages and disadvantages and which you do will, in part, be influenced by how you built your greenhouse floor.

Growing in The Ground

Some people like to grow in the ground because it saves money on containers and compost. If you haven't paved or concreted your entire greenhouse floor, then this is a practical method of growing.

The advantages of this method are:

- No need to buy containers or compost
- Cheap and easy to get started on

The disadvantages of this method are:

- Pests and diseases can easily build up in the soil, particularly in smaller greenhouses
- The top soil will need regularly changing to reduce this risk and to replenish nutrients
- Weeds will grow in the soil giving you extra work
- Potential for water build up if the soil doesn't drain freely
- Very easy to damage your greenhouse or move the foundation when digging over the soil
- Gives pests and rodents an easy way into your greenhouse in the cooler months
- Unable to move plants around to take advantage of the sun or shade

My personal opinion is that this method is not a good way to grow plants in a greenhouse. You are immediately faced with lots of problems, and you are increasing your workload significantly.

Growing in Containers

This is preferred by most greenhouse growers because it massively reduces their workload.

The advantages of this method are:

- Easy crop rotation
- Can move plants around to take advantage of sunny/shady areas
- No weeding

- Far fewer pests
- Greenhouse looks neater and is easier to manage
- Easy to remove diseased plants
- Easy to put plants outside on hotter days

The disadvantages of this method are:

- Higher initial cost for greenhouse flooring
- Need to buy compost every year
- Must clean containers every winter or buy new ones

For me, this is the best way of growing in a greenhouse because you have less work to do and can take advantage of all the positive points of greenhouse gardening.

In some greenhouses, you can get away with a good quality plastic woven weed membrane as the floor which will keep your costs down. Just be aware that this will need to be replaced every couple of years and should be regularly swept to prevent the build-up of soil on it and the associated problems.

Containers are the way forward unless you have very specific reasons for growing in the ground. The extra work and risk to your plants just simply isn't worth it to save a little bit of money on your greenhouse floor.

SECURING YOUR GREENHOUSE AGAINST THE WIND

One of the biggest dangers your greenhouse faces is the wind. A high wind can rip a greenhouse to pieces, twisting the frame and shattering the glass, so you need to take steps to protect your precious greenhouse and the plants inside.

Firstly, you need to make sure that all the panes of glass are securely in place and none are broken. A corner missing out of a pane can give the wind ingress to then blow out other panes and damage your greenhouse. Although a greenhouse isn't a completely sealed unit, solid panes will help to protect it from wind damage.

You can buy a galvanized steel base for your greenhouse, which usually comes as a flat pack. Although not essential these are extremely helpful as the base will raise up your greenhouse a little and helps make it more stable because you can secure the base to the foundation and the greenhouse to the base.

A greenhouse base is secured to the foundation by pushing specially designed metal hooks into pockets of wet concrete which are then secured to the frame. An alternative fixing is to lay a concrete strip that sits under the greenhouse base. Drilling then secures the base as it is bolted it to the concrete.

One of the favorite ways to secure a greenhouse is to lay a single course of bricks on a concrete footing and then secure the greenhouse to the bricks without using a greenhouse base. In some cases, you may want to use wooden batons between the greenhouse and the bricks.

Of course, you can dramatically reduce the potential for damage simply by locating your greenhouse in a more sheltered area. The trouble is you often have to balance sun exposure with shelter, but you will have to make that judgment call based on your knowledge of your site.

Although you can do everything possible to protect your greenhouse, no matter what you do you cannot make it complete stormproof. There will also be cases where a freak storm hits. If severe weather warnings are given for your area, then you should probably remove any plants you want to save to another location where they will be protected during the storm.

If your greenhouse is square and level, then it is more likely to have better fitting glass. Loose glass will rattle, and this has much more chance of breaking. The gaps in a non-square frame allows the wind into the greenhouse where it can cause all sorts of destruction.

Most greenhouses will have a flexible rubber glazing seal between the glass and the aluminum frame. These have a tendency to perish over time and will frequently disappear when moving a greenhouse. These seals hold the glass in place and prevents the wind getting into your greenhouse. Regularly check your seals and replace them if they start to perish. It will go a long way to protecting your greenhouse from wind damage.

Glazing clips hold the glass to the frame, and these have a habit of vanishing. They pop off during wind storms, get knocked off and generally vanish. You should check the glazing clips at least once a year to make sure they are in place. If any are missing, then they should be replaced as soon as possible.

Both of these items are relatively cheap and easy to find. You will typically find the best prices online on sites such as eBay.

If high winds or a storm are forecast then you should make sure that all vents, windows, and doors are shut. Although automatic vents are a wonderful thing, if they open up during a storm it could end up destroying your greenhouse, so turn them off for the duration!

If you live in a particularly windy area, then you may want to consider putting up a windbreak to protect your greenhouse. It may be worthwhile sacrificing some sunshine for protection from the wind.

Siting a greenhouse so the prevailing wind flows over it rather than hits one end is another method of reducing the potential for wind damage.

Another option is to replace your horticultural glass with toughened safety glass. This is stronger so is harder to break. It comes in larger panes so you do not have smaller, overlapping panes. Also, if there is any damage then toughened glass is much easier to clean up than horticultural glass.

Most greenhouses will use glass clips to hold the glass in place, but you can use bar capping or continuous strip fixings which are stronger and are less likely to give in high winds.

One of your prime considerations when siting and building your greenhouse has to be to protect it from damage in the wind. A greenhouse is a significant investment in both time and money and should it get wrecked you could lose your seedlings or crops. Before you begin erecting your greenhouse understand the wind patterns in your area and site your greenhouse in the best location you can to reduce the impact of the wind.

ESSENTIAL GREENHOUSE EQUIPMENT

There are a lot of gadgets and gizmos you can buy for your greenhouse and what you end up buying will depend not only on your budget but on what you are planning to grow in your greenhouse.

To make the best use of the space, you will need some form of greenhouse staging. This makes it easier for you to work plus you can get more plants in your greenhouse. When you are starting off your seedlings, this will be very important as you will need a lot of space!

You can buy greenhouse staging though it is quite easy to make your own and not as expensive as you might think! With some wooden pallets and 2x1" battens, you can easily make a greenhouse bench that is the right height for you. If you are taller or shorter than normal, then this is a real benefit as it will reduce back ache massively!

Build the staging to about 4 feet (120cm) long, 2 feet (60cm) deep and about 3 feet (90cm) high. Ideally, you want two shelves though if you can make the bottom shelf removable, it means you can take the shelf out as your plants grow and give yourself more space for plants!

The thick battens from the pallets are used to make the legs while the planks at used as the shelves. The 2x1" wood is used for straps and stringers. Although it does take time to build, it is cheaper than buying staging.

If you are planning on moving your staging regularly, then you may want to buy aluminum staging as it is lighter.

There are plenty of different types of greenhouse bench to buy in the stores from both single and double shelf models. You can also buy all sorts of specialist staging including orchid staging and raised bed grow bag stands!

Ultimately it depends on your individual needs as to what type of staging you need, but the normal double shelf staging should do the job just fine for most of us.

In the spring time, you will often find yourself overwhelmed with seed trays. You can buy seed tray racks which allow you to stack seed trays vertically, which helps you to make the most of your space. These aren't cheap, but as an alternative some kitchen cupboard stacking space savers or plant stands will make good seed tray stackers at a fraction of the price!

One area that is often considered wasted space is the area in the eaves of your greenhouse. However, some bright spark has come up with a solution for that problem, and you can buy shelving that fits to your roof bars with adjustable brackets. One advantage of this type of shelving is that as heat rises plants kept there tend to be warmer!

There are a lot of other gadgets and gizmos you can use in your greenhouse, and we have talked about irrigation systems, heating systems, and fans earlier in this book.

Ultimately though, the equipment you need for your greenhouse will depend on exactly what you are using it for. I have staging along one side of my greenhouse which has two levels of shelving which I use for storage and growing seedlings on. The other side of my greenhouse has no shelving, and here I grow taller plants like cucumelon, tomato and tromboncino squashes which grow very tall.

Don't go out and buy equipment just because you feel you need to have it. As you start to use your greenhouse, so you will learn what equipment you need and then you can go out and buy it. That way you are not cluttering your greenhouse up with unnecessary equipment, but you are also saving yourself money!

STARTING SEEDLINGS IN YOUR GREENHOUSE

One of the biggest benefits of a greenhouse is it gives you somewhere to start your seedlings off, so you get a head start on the growing season. I always used to start mine on windowsills, but my wife never appreciated me moving the ornaments and family photos to do so. Not to mention that the cats would sit on them, eat them or just knock them off and get soil on the carpet.

Even a small, plastic portable greenhouse out in your garden is sufficient to start your seeds off, and the extra warmth means you can get a really good head start on the year.

Germinating seeds is something many of us will do every year, but it is often touch and go as to whether or not they will germinate. It can be hard to find enough space to germinate all the seeds that you want to plant, and you end up not planting some crops you wanted to grow.

A greenhouse is a real boon because it gives you plenty of space to start your seeds in a protected environment.

Firstly, you will need your seeds which you will probably have a lot of already but will undoubtedly (as we all do) order more every year. Although you can buy these from eBay, it is usually worth buying them from reputable and known sellers, so you know exactly what you are getting. I have bought seeds off eBay and had very poor germination rates, or they haven't been the seeds I've expected.

Personally, I now buy from big brand online retailers or local shops because I know exactly what I am getting. If you buy seeds for the following year at the end of the growing season, then you can usually get them on sale and save yourself some money.

You then need a decent growing medium. A good, peat based seed compost is a good place to start though you can mix up your own formulas. Avoid cheap compost because it tends to dry out very quickly, have large lumps in and not be as good for your seedlings. You can find your seeds rot before they germinate because the cheap compost doesn't drain well.

Seed trays and containers are good to get, and I often use ones with plastic lids. This way I can have a greenhouse within a greenhouse or I can use the plastic lid as I am hardening off the seedlings.

There are a huge variety of seed trays on the market, and I use a combination of open trays and trays with cells. Depending on what I am growing I will use different seed trays. Larger cell trays are used for larger plants whereas open trays are used for seeds that can be scattered like beetroot, carrot and so on.

For some seeds, such as sweetcorn cardboard tubes (such as those found inside toilet rolls) are good to use because the seedlings do not like being handled. The tubes can be planted straight in the ground, and the cardboard will rot as the seedling grows.

Larger plants such as squashes are best sown in individual pots so they can grow to a decent size without having to be re-potted, which they can object to.

You can use peat pots to grow your seedlings in though I have found these have a habit of either drying out too much or becoming sodden and then rotting. Some people like these but I'm not keen on them.

All of these can be sat in seed trays to make it easier for you to organize your plants. Just remember that you have to prick out your seedlings and re-pot them when they get to a certain size and certain types of plants will not appreciate this.

Heat mats can be used to help with germination, but they are not necessary. If you live in a really cold climate, then they are a benefit, but it does require that you have electricity in your greenhouse, which not everyone will have. You also have the expense of buying the heat mats so you may get one or two to start off your most important or delicate seedlings.

I have a hydroponic system with grow lamps at home which I use to start off seedlings like tomatoes and pumpkins. These are then transplanted to pots and put in the greenhouse where they continue to flourish.

You need to think about the light requirements of each plant because some seedlings prefer more light to others. More sun sensitive seedlings will need shading from the heat of the midday sun.

One useful technique when sowing seeds in individual pots is to place two or three seeds into each pot, spaced out evenly. This way if one or two seeds do not germinate you still have a third which could grow. If all three grow, then you can either prick out and re-plant the three seedlings, or you can discard the smaller seedlings, keeping the strongest.

All seeds need to be covered by the growing medium but not too deeply otherwise they will not push through the soil to the light. Check the packets to determine exactly how deeply to plant each seed.

For bigger seeds, it is easy to poke them into the soil. One thing to remember with larger seeds such as squash seeds is to plant them on their sides so they can grow the right way up. If they are put in the ground the wrong way, then you can find the roots coming up through the soil and the leaves growing underground! This often happens when children help with the planting.

For smaller seeds, you need to cover them with a sprinkling of soil to stop them blowing away. With smaller seeds, you will need to be careful watering them as they can float away with excess water!

Seeds can take anything from a few days to a few weeks for them to germinate, depending on the type of plant you are growing. Check the packet for specific timings, so you know when to start checking your seedlings.

During this time, you need to keep them moist, but not wet otherwise the seeds can rot. Check the pots regularly and make sure they are not too damp. Peat pots can go moldy if the humidity is too high so you need to keep an eye on them too.

When you plant your seeds will depend on the type of plant you are growing. Check the instructions and plant during the time they state. Remember that with a greenhouse you can start your seedlings earlier in cooler areas than you can outside.

Hardening Off

Not all of your seedlings are going to spend their lives in your greenhouse; some will be planted outside. Moving a plant from the protective enclosure that is your greenhouse into the great outdoors can be an incredible shock to the system. The difference in environments causes shock which can at best stunt the growth of your plant by several weeks, and at worst kill it!

Hardening off your seedlings is vital if you want them to survive and thrive when you plant them outside of your greenhouse. You will be surprised how many people don't do this and struggle to get their plants to grow.

The process of hardening off isn't done overnight and can take a week or two, depending on the weather where you live. You will have to be patient, but it is worth it as it strengthens your plants and ensures they grow well.

Once there is no risk of frost during the day you take your seedlings out of your greenhouse and leave them outside during the day. Put them somewhere that is warm but not too sunny, and that is sheltered from the wind.

Leave your seedlings outside for most of the day and then mid to late afternoon move them back into your greenhouse.

Repeat this for two or three days and then gradually move them into sunnier locations and leave them out for longer.

After a couple of weeks, the seedlings should be in the location where they are to be planted and be left out all day and throughout the night.

Should your plants show any sign of stress such as browning, wilting or yellowing then move the hardening process back a step and try again the following day.

Water well during this process and then after the two weeks, you should be able to plant your seedlings out in the ground. It is worth keeping a close eye on them as some may benefit from horticultural fleece or a cloche if the weather starts to get cold or if there is a surprise frost.

Sorting Your Seed Packets

Most gardeners will have seeds packets pretty much everywhere, in drawers, on shelves, tucked away in cupboards. They accumulate, and it is far too easy to get overwhelmed by them. You know what it is like, you get halfway through the growing season and realize you forgot to plant something because you couldn't find the seeds!

There are plenty of different ways for you to organize your seed packets and it is up to you how best you do it. However, I would strongly recommend that you do organize them because it will make your life easier throughout the growing season and save you money from buying duplicate seed packets.

I have created an organizational system which works for me. I'll share it with you, and you can use it yourself or adjust it to suit what you grow.

43

Firstly, I sort the seeds into three piles:
1. Herbs
2. Flowers
3. Vegetables

These are stored separately.

The packets are then put into a large container and ordered in a very specific way. I put dividers (usually made of cardboard) into the container on which I write each month of the year.

Each seed packet is filed under the first month in which it can be planted. So if I can sow my leeks in February, then they are put in the February section. Within each section, you can organize the seeds alphabetically if it helps you!

For me, this is the best way to organize my seeds because I know that in January I can look at my January seeds and decide what to plant (assuming I don't have a plan for the year). It makes my life easier because I am not sorting through piles of seeds trying to work out what I should be planting.

This is my method and it works very well for me. It keeps me a little bit more organized and saves time when it comes to deciding what to plant. If you find a different system works for you, then by all means use that.

Remember that if a seed packet states it can be planted out in a month, then you can often start the seedling off in a greenhouse between four and eight weeks earlier, depending on whether it is heated or not!

A greenhouse is a real boon when it comes to starting off seedlings and will help you get a head start on the growing season. It also gets the seed trays out of the house and gives your plants a great start in life.

Growing Tomatoes

One of the most popular plants to grow in a greenhouse is tomatoes. These have quite a long growing season, and for many of us in cooler climates, there simply isn't enough time for them to ripen outside every year. With a greenhouse though you can start your tomato plants earlier in the year and extend your growing season so that the tomato plants can ripen.

In this chapter, we will talk specifically about growing tomatoes in a greenhouse, but you can learn more about growing tomatoes in my book "Growing Tomatoes: Your Guide to Growing Delicious Tomatoes at Home" available on Amazon.

Tomatoes are a great greenhouse crop, but you need to look after the plants and give them a lot of attention because they will grow like crazy and soon take over your greenhouse. I always remember growing tomatoes for the first time in a greenhouse. I went away for two weeks in the middle of the growing season and came home to find the plants literally bursting out of the greenhouse!

You will typically start tomatoes off quite early on in the season, particularly if your greenhouse is heated, which virtually eliminates the risk of frost damage.

Usually, tomato seeds are planted around March, which is about six weeks before the last frost date in the United Kingdom. It will vary depending on how far north you are. In warmer climates, you can grow tomatoes pretty much all year in a greenhouse! If you need to know the last frost date in your area, then there are plenty of websites that can calculate this for you.

Typically, you will start your seedlings six weeks before the last frost date and then plant outside a week or so after the date to avoid a surprise frost. Of course, this is not so much of a problem growing in your greenhouse as you are not beholden to the seasons, particularly if your greenhouse is heated.

Tomato Varieties

There are a few different types of tomato plant which grow in different ways. It's important that you understand these types as it influences how you look after the plants

.Determinate varieties are better known as bush tomatoes and so don't need the side shoots pinching out. These tomatoes are hardier and well suited for later planting. However, because they take up less space, they are very well suited for a greenhouse because space is at a premium. Determinate tomatoes tend to produce their crop all at once rather than fruiting throughout the growing season. If you stagger the planting times, you can get a continuous supply of tomatoes.

Indeterminate tomatoes will appreciate a greenhouse, but they have a habit of getting out of control very quickly. These are the plants where you need to remove the side shoots and pinch the tops off otherwise they continue to grow! Cherry and plum tomatoes are great as an indeterminate variety, and this type of tomato does produce a substantial crop, more so than a determinate variety. However, indeterminate tomatoes will require a lot more attention. They will take over your greenhouse if you don't keep them under control!

Growing Tomatoes from Seeds

There is a fair split between people who start their tomatoes from seeds and those who buy pre-grown seedlings. The advantage of the latter is that you don't have the hassle of germinating your tomatoes and they are handy in case of seed failure. The downside of them is that the number of varieties you will find are very limited.

If you want some of the more unusual, and some would argue the tastiest tomatoes, then you will have to buy them as seeds.

There are thousands of different varieties of tomatoes available, so you need to choose the specific types you want to grow. Think about the size of greenhouse you have and the type of tomatoes you like to eat.

When starting your seeds off, it is better to start them in a 3-4" (7-10cm) pot which is wide enough for the seedling to spread its roots and grow to a decent size. It means less transplanting of vulnerable seedlings and less risk of damage to your precious plants.

Fill the pots with a good quality seed compost, leaving about a ½" (1cm) space. Put a single seed in the top of the pot and cover it with a thin layer of soil. Remember to label your pots if you are planting more than one variety of tomato.

Put the pots in your greenhouse where they will get at least four hours of direct sun each day. The warmer the environment and the more sunlight the seeds get, then the quicker they will germinate. Heat lamps and mats will help speed up germination, but they do require your greenhouse to have electricity.

Covering your pots with plastic bags or plastic wrap to form a small greenhouse around each pot will help with germination, but you need to keep a close eye on the seeds. At the first sign of germination, the plastic should be removed. If it is left on too long, then the plants will die from a lack of air circulation and will suffer from damping off disease and rot.

Overwatering your seeds will also cause problems as the seeds will rot. When the topsoil looks dry, sprinkle enough water on it just to moisten it rather than soaking it with your watering can.

With most tomato varieties the seeds will germinate within around two weeks, though some varieties will take a little longer. Within 6 to 8 weeks the seedlings will be large enough to transfer to larger pots. Make sure that there is sufficient air flow between the plants and use horticultural fleece to keep them warm.

Some people will plant four or five seeds in each pot and then transplant them when they are about an inch (2-3cm) tall to individual pots. Be very careful when you are transplanting them as they are delicate. Damaging the roots could stunt the growth, and it is very easy to damage the stalk or leaves. It depends on the space in your greenhouse as to whether you do this or plant singularly.

When the seedlings are about 8" (20cm) tall, they can be transplanted on to their final location. If this is outdoors, then make sure it is warm enough to plant them out and ensure you have hardened them off first.

If your tomato plants are staying in pots, then make sure the pots are large enough so that you will not need to re-pot your plants in the future. Determinate (bush) varieties need a minimum pot size of 6 liters whereas indeterminate varieties will need at least 10 liters. Make sure there are sufficient drainage holes; lots of smaller holes are better than one big hole so drill your own if necessary.

Positioning Your Tomatoes
Your plants need to get as much sunshine as they can in your greenhouse, but it is vital that the plants aren't overcrowded.

Tomatoes must have space between the plants so that the air can circulate. If not, then the plants become susceptible to fungal diseases, and you run the risk of losing your crops.

This need of air circulation is one reason why many people will grow determinate varieties in their greenhouse. Because the plants are smaller, they are much easier to space properly and are less likely to get out of control like the indeterminate varieties. I cannot stress how important this is for a successful crop.

Growing Tomatoes in Grow Bags
Grow bags have become quite popular as a way to grow along the borders of your greenhouse without using the soil or pots. You use the grow bag for a season and then discard or compost the contents of the grow bag.

As with potting compost, it is important to buy good quality grow bags. There are cheap grow bags on the market, and sometimes your budget will limit you to these. If you can, though, it is worth buying the more expensive grow bags as they typically have better quality compost in, retain moisture better and provide food for your tomato plants for longer.

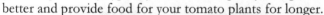

Grow bags are usually solid lumps of compost wh
before you plant in them you should break up the soil
of your tomato plants grow. All you do is put the g'
its side and bash it a bit! Be careful not to puncture u.

A typical grow bag is large enough to hold three tom...
the pre-marked areas on the top and then plant your tomatoes .
sure the root balls are fully covered with compost.

Although grow bags are useful they can be difficult to grow
indeterminate tomato varieties in because it is hard to support the plants.
You can buy support frames designed for use with grow bags. The
traditional bamboo cane can be used but as your plants grow tall they will
not provide enough support and the plants will topple over.

Cordon Tomatoes

This refers to indeterminate tomatoes where the stem grows without side
branches.

Indeterminate varieties of tomato grow like crazy. You have the main
stem, which grows out of the roots and then the trusses or leaf stems which
grow out from the main stem. The trusses are where the flowers set (you'll
hear the term "set trusses" in relation to growing tomatoes) and the fruit
forms.

Suckers or side shoots grow out from between the main stem and a leaf
stem in indeterminate tomatoes. If left to their own devices these will grow
and produce flowers, fruit, and more side shoots. You may think this is a
great thing, but unfortunately, the tomato plant will sink all of its energy
into producing all of this greenery and not get around to producing any
fruit!

These side shoots must be removed. Simply pinch them out using your
thumb and forefinger and discard them. The best tomato crops are
produced when the plant is cordoned, i.e. the side shoots are pinched off.

ou will have to keep on doing this throughout the growing season as
ur plants will produce these side shoots rapidly. They will also send out
uckers from near the root ball which must be removed.

Determinate varieties though do not need these side shoots removed
and can be left alone.

Stopping Tomatoes

One other thing you need to do is make sure your tomato plants do not
grow too tall as they will happily produce lots of greenery and very few
flowers given half a chance.

Indeterminate tomatoes need to be stopped or topped to prevent them
growing too large. Determinate tomatoes do not need this done.

When your plant has grown between four and six trusses (leaf stems),
then you need to stop its upward growth. Depending on the size of your
greenhouse, the number of tomato plants you have and the length of your
growing season you will decide how tall to let your plants grow. Going over
six trusses isn't recommended as your plant may struggle to produce a ripe
crop.

Cut the main stem of the tomato around two leaves above the top stem.
This will divert the plant's energy into fruiting, but it will also keep trying to
produce side shoots which will need removing.

Feeding Your Tomatoes

This is surprisingly easy and relies on you remembering you do it more than
anything else!

If you are using grow bags, then for the first 3 to 6 weeks (depending on
the grow-bag) you won't need to feed your plants during this time.

Start by using a high nitrogen liquid fertilizer, diluted according to the
instructions on the bottle. Use this once a week as the nitrogen encourages
healthy leaf growth.

When the first tomatoes have started to set then switch to using a
fertilizer that is high in both potash and potassium which will encourage
fruit growth.

You can buy specific tomato feeds which are okay to use. These
fertilizers are specifically formulated to give tomatoes what they need. For
extra special tomatoes, you should look at using the two different feeds
though as it will encourage far better growth.

Watering Your Tomatoes

As a rough rule of thumb, a tomato plant in a greenhouse will need about a
liter of water every day. In hot weather, they will need more and in cooler
weather, less.

Daily light watering is much better for your plants than giving them a good drenching every now and again. The latter unfortunately will lead to your tomatoes splitting and cracking.

It's easy to check whether your tomatoes need water. Stick your forefinger into the soil to the second knuckle. If it feels moist at your finger tip, then the plant doesn't need water. If it feels dry, then water your plants.

Be aware that a plant which is overwatered exhibits very similar symptoms to one which is too dry, so it is best to check the soil.

Common Pests and Diseases

One of the biggest dangers your tomato plants face is blight. This will wipe out your plants quickly. However, blight is a wind born fungal infection, and in a greenhouse, you are much less likely to encounter this.

Red Spider Mites

These are almost impossible to see with the naked eye but are a common problem with greenhouse grown tomatoes.

If the top of the leaves starts to become mottled, bronzed or speckled, then there is a problem. Try to cool the plants and mist the underside of the leaves (where the mites live) with water.

Your local garden store will sell a predatory mite called *Phytoselius Persimilis* which will eat the pesky red spider mites.

Don't use pesticides as they don't work against red spider mites and will just kill off the beneficial insects.

Whitefly

Another major irritation in your greenhouse these start off in spring as small, 1½mm scaly crawlers which then become tiny white moths.

These are pretty common in greenhouses so being proactive is important and will head off a lot of problems at the pass, so to speak.

If you suffer from whitefly then at the beginning of April introduce *Encarsia Formosa*, which is a parasitic wasp, into your greenhouse. This will helpfully eat the young whitefly.

Towards the end of April hang some fly catching sheets around your tomato plants to catch the adult whitefly.

Unfortunately, most whiteflies are resistant to pesticides, and the sprays which are effective are very strong and will be absorbed by your tomatoes and therefore by you when you eat them.

Growing tomatoes in a greenhouse is a really good use of the space. Tomatoes have quite a long growing season and require heat rather than sunlight to ripen, which they get in a greenhouse. If you live in a temperate zone, a greenhouse is almost vital to get a good crop of tomatoes, particularly with the variable weather many of us have been experiencing over recent years.

GROWING CHILIES & BELL PEPPERS

Another popular greenhouse crop is peppers, both bell peppers, and chili peppers. For many people, these cannot be grown outside as they require a long, warm growing season. Also for a chili connoisseur, growing your own is essential as few of the hotter, more interesting peppers are available to buy in stores.

These plants like a warm, sunny and sheltered position. Unfortunately, unless you happen to live in one of the warmer countries or states, you are going to struggle to grow these to maturity outside.

Pepper plants like a well-drained, nutrient rich and moisture retaining soil which is slightly on the acidic side. As you are growing in a greenhouse, you are most likely going to be growing either in pots or grow bags. If you mix well-rotted manure into your compost, the plants will appreciate it but avoid fresh manure as it is high in nitrogen which encourages excessive leaf growth.

When growing chilies, most growers will start their plants off from seeds. Bell peppers and the more common chili varieties are found as seedlings in garden stores.

The plants are ready for planting in their final position when they reach flowering size, which is typically after about eight weeks.

You need to space your plants between 15 and 18 inches apart (38-45cm), so there is plenty of space between them to allow for air circulation. Most grow-bags will easily hold three pepper plants, but they run the risk of drying out so need to be regularly checked and watered. Mulching your grow-bags will help the soil retain water.

Once the first fruit has set, then you can start to feed the plants with a liquid fertilizer. Choose one high in potassium to help fruit development and feed once a week.

Pepper plants will tolerate the temperature dropping to 54F/12C at night, but if you can keep the temperature about 59F/15C, then your plants will produce a better crop. Use bubble wrap and horticultural fleece if you don't have any heating in your greenhouse.

If the temperature rises above 86F/30C, then this can reduce your yield.

Peppers like a humid atmosphere and will benefit from the greenhouse being damped down a couple of times a day in hotter weather.

Harvesting Your Crop

If you pick peppers when they are green, then you will encourage further growth. If you leave the peppers on the plant, they will change color. Bell peppers will sweeten while chilies will get hotter.

Leaving the fruit on the plants will stop further flowers developing, which will result in the yield being reduced by about 25%.

For many home growers, the sweeter or hotter fruit is worth the reduced yield. You can expect to harvest your first fruits towards the end of July and the start of August.

If you leave the fruits on the plant at the end of the season, they will shrivel up and dry. Most people though will pick the fruits and dry them themselves.

Pruning Your Pepper Plants

Pepper plants will naturally branch into at least two stems, producing flower buds at the joints. You can encourage more side shoots to be produced by pinching out shoots at about a foot long.

For plants with high yields or those grown in grow bags stakes are recommended to prevent the stems from breaking. Use multiple canes to provide a good level of support as the stems are quite brittle.

Propagation

Seeds are sown from the middle of February to the start of April for greenhouse growing.

The best temperature for seed germination is between 18C and 22C (64-71F). They will benefit from a heating mat to keep the temperature within this range.

If your greenhouse is not heated, then start your seeds off mid to late

March.

The seeds should be sown thinly in moist compost in a propagator. Be careful not to over-water your seeds as they can rot or get swept away with the excess water. The compost needs to be moist, not soggy; an important distinction.

Once the seeds have germinated and set two true leaves, you can then re-pot them into 3" (75mm) pots and grow them on.

After they have reached about a foot high, they will have developed a strong root system and should be potted on to their final position.

Watering Your Plants

Pepper plants hate irregular watering and will drop flowers and fruits if they are not getting enough water. However, overwatering your plants is just as damaging because the plants need to be able to access oxygen by the roots, which a wet soil stops them from doing.

Pepper plants are thirsty plants, and during hot weather, they will need watering twice a day. They do benefit from irrigation systems.

The key to producing a good yield is to water your plants little and often.

Caring for Your Plants

Start by staking your plants out with small stakes when you pot them on to their final position. As the plants grow taller, swap the stakes for canes to provide better support.

One issue you can face growing peppers in a greenhouse is pollination. Even leaving windows and vents open may not attract enough pollinating insects to your plants.

You can help pollinate your flowers by wetting a small paint brush. Gently paint the inside of each of your flowers to spread the pollen between the flowers so they produce fruit.

Potential Problems

Pepper plants of all types are most commonly attacked by red spider mites, whitefly and aphids when growing in greenhouses. Biological controls, such as those discussed in the previous chapter, are effective.

Grey mold can be an issue if your plants are too close together. Remove any diseased material and improve air circulation. Overwatering and poor spacing will encourage rot and mold which will cause a lot of damage in your greenhouse to all of your plants, not just your peppers.

Slugs and Snails

Slugs and snails love chili and pepper plants. Watch out for slime trails and nibbled fruits or leaves. Keeping your greenhouse clear of debris, pots and other hiding places will help keep the pest population down. You can try other techniques like coffee ground, copper rings, crushed egg shells but in my experience, these aren't always that effective.

Visiting your greenhouse at dusk or dawn will find slugs and snails at their most active so you can pick them off and destroy them. Alternatively, slug pellets are very effective and often the best way to keep these voracious eaters under control.

Aphids

Aphids are another common problem in a greenhouse and will infect your pepper plants very quickly. They will usually gather at the shoot tips, on the young leaves, and the flower buds. They look like tiny white flecks and often attract ants which farm them for food.

A simple solution is to spray your plants with a weak soap solution as this kills aphids.

Attracting ladybirds and hoverflies into your greenhouse will also kill them off as they prey on the pests. Planting marigolds in and around your greenhouse will help attract these beneficial predators.

Harvesting Your Chilies

Fruits are typically ready from July to September and are harvested using a sharp knife or scissors. Cut through the stem just above the chili and then store or use your chili as you wish.

Before the first frost, you should harvest all the fruits from your chili plants. Remove the branches and hang them upside down, which will allow the fruits to continue to mature.

Unripe peppers can be ripened off the plant as they will not overwinter. Put them in a paper bag with a ripe banana which will give off ethylene gas which ripens fruit.

Overwintering Your Chilies

It is possible to get larger yields from your chili plant by overwintering them, i.e. providing a protective environment for your plant in the coldest months.

Between October and January, the plants will grow very little. You need to be careful not to overwater your plants during this time and to keep them safe from frosts. Check the soil carefully before watering as you may only need to water your plants once every two or three weeks!

A heated greenhouse is going to be necessary for many areas, but with bubble wrap and horticultural fleece, your plants may be ok in all but the coldest of areas. Alternatively, you can bring them into your house and put them on a sunny windowsill.

In their second year, your plants will produce a much larger crop as they have a head start when the light and the sun returns in the spring.

Most chili growers will only overwinter the strongest plants as weaker plants are much more likely to die in the colder months.

As the leaves start to drop from the plant, prune it back leaving around 4 to 6 inches (10-15cm) of the main stem.

Plants grown in the ground will need lifting carefully and potting up in fresh compost.

Overwintered pepper plants need to be kept at a temperature of between 5C and 12C (41-54F). If the temperature rises above 12C/54F, then the plant will start to grow, which you don't want to happen until spring time.

When spring comes and the weather warms up, your plants are going to start to grow again. At this point, temperature becomes very important, and sudden cold snaps can cause a lot of problems for your precious plants.

From the end of February or start of March, as the days lengthen you want to keep your plants at a temperature of around 22C if you can. If your greenhouse is not heated, then you need to keep your plants above 12C, so they continue to grow.

When the risk of frost has passed, you can plant your pepper plants back outside if that is where you are growing them.

Bell pepper and chili pepper plants are very popular plants to grow in a greenhouse. Needed hot weather and with a long growing season many gardeners simply cannot grow them successfully outside. They are a very successful greenhouse crop and will do well whether in a heated or unheated greenhouse.

GROWING CITRUS PLANTS

Citrus plants are another popular plant to grow in greenhouses. Whether you grow them in the greenhouse all year round or just overwinter them, a greenhouse can help keep these delicate plants alive and thriving.

There are a huge variety of citrus plants on the market, and they usually grow in warmer environments such as around the Mediterranean. They grow best in a temperature range of 70-90F (21-32C) and are not frost tolerant.

As citrus trees grow into full-size trees naturally you either want to buy a dwarf cultivar or make sure your plant becomes pot bound, so it doesn't grow too big.

They do have particular soil and food requirements, needing a different food in winter to summer. It is very important that you stick to a good feeding and watering cycle as they are very susceptible to leaf or fruit drop from lack of water.

Typically, you will water your citrus trees when the top three inches of soil is dry. They benefit from irrigation as citrus plants will drop both leaves and fruit if they dry out too much.

In winter citrus plants require less water as their growth slows in these cooler months. Winter is also the time to prune your citrus plants, removing any weak or damaged branches.

The nice thing about citrus plants is that in virtually all areas you can put them outside in summer. As you grow them in pots when the risk of frost has passed, you can put them outside in a sheltered but sunny position from the middle of June until late September. If there are any sudden cold nights, then fleece them or put them back in your greenhouse. This frees up space in your greenhouse when you most need to for your other plants to expand and grow.

Different citrus plants will tolerate different night time temperatures. Most lemon trees will be happy down to about 50F/10C though kumquats can tolerate temperatures as low as 45F/7C. Check the labels of any plants you buy, so you know the exact minimum night-time temperature they will tolerate.

Most citrus plants are self-fertile, again check the labels, and so a single plant will produce fruit. In a pot, you can expect the tree to grow to 3 to 5 feet (1-1.5m) tall.

One word of advice with citrus plants though. They do not like being in centrally heated rooms. The rooms tend to be too hot, not humid enough and cause stress in citrus plants. This results in them dropping leaves and fruit and dying, and is the reason why many people who try to grow citrus trees fail!

Feeding Your Citrus Plants

These plants are considered to be hungry plants, requiring regular feeding. In summer (end of March to October) you will give them a high nitrogen feed. Although you can buy a winter feed for citrus plants in most cases, you will not need to water them. As the temperatures drop, they become dormant, and so require fewer nutrients.

Watering Your Citrus Plants

In the hotter months, they will benefit from a good amount of watering. If you can use rainwater, then do so, as they do prefer it. In winter time let the surface partially dry out before you water it. Then water thoroughly using tepid rainwater; cold water can produce root shock and cause problems for your plants.

One of the most common problems citrus plants face in winter is over watering. Because they are dormant, they do not need as much water, and people keep to the summer watering schedule, which results in the plant dying.

Although growing citrus plants in a centrally heated room is harder, you can help them by increasing the humidity. Stand the pot on a tray filled with gravel and then fill the tray with water up to the gravel level. Combine this with misting the leaves early in the morning, and the plant should be happy enough with the humidity levels to grow.

Repotting Your Citrus Plants

Your citrus plants will appreciate being repotted every year around the middle of March. If you are not repotting the plant completely, then remove the top 2" (5cm) of compost and replace it with fresh compost.

Pruning Citrus Plants

Citrus plants don't require a lot of pruning. In February you can thin out overcrowded branches and trim back leggy plants by as much as two-thirds! If you cut back the tallest branch at this time, it will also encourage bushy growth.

During the summer months, you can pinch out the tips of the most vigorous shoots using your thumb and forefinger. This, again, will encourage the plant to become bushier and therefore produce more fruit.

One thing to watch out for with citrus plants is the production of "water shoots." These are fast growing shoots which appear from the main stem of the plant, usually the bottom half of the stem. They can appear from below the graft point too.

If you see any of these, then remove the shoots immediately as they won't produce any fruit and will just drain the resources of your plant.

Citrus trees are fun to grow and very unusual. Whatever variety you choose to grow you can keep it in your greenhouse in the colder months. If the greenhouse is not heated, then it will need fleecing to protect it if the temperature drops too low, but come summer you can move it outside and enjoy a harvest of fresh citrus fruits!

GROWING SQUASHES

Squash plants such as pumpkin, marrow, butternut squash, Turk's turban and many more can be grown in a greenhouse. Most of us will grow them outside, but in colder areas, with shorter growing seasons they will need the protection of a greenhouse or polytunnel.

For many of us though, a greenhouse provides a protective environment to start your squash plants off in before you plant them out after the risk of frost has passed.

Squash plants grow to an enormous size so if you do not have a large greenhouse you should look for a dwarf or smaller variety, so it doesn't take up too much space. If you are planning on growing your plants outside after the seedlings are established, the choice of variety is much greater.

You can train squash plants to grow up and over the roof of your greenhouse, providing some shade for other plants. However, do consider that they will grow like crazy so you may have to pinch out the ends as well as any side shoots to prevent them growing too large and crowding out your other plants.

When you start your seeds off will depend on when the last frost date is in your area and the type of squash plant you are growing. Check the packets for exact information, but typically squash plants are sown from the end of March until the end of May.

Start the seed off in a pot about 3" across, sowing one seed to each pot. The seed should be sown about an inch deep in the soil. You can sow two seeds per pot and then thin out the weaker of the two seedlings.

Sow the seed on its side because they do have a right way up! Planting the seed the wrong way up will result in the roots growing upwards and the leaves growing into the soil (seriously this is true). This commonly happens when children help, and the plant can be rescued and turned the right way up if spotted in time.

Once you see roots coming out of the bottom of the pot, then you need to move the plant to a larger pot. Be very careful because the seedlings are very delicate. As they have a habit of trailing, it can be very easy to break or damage the stems. I broke the stem one year on one of the only squash plants I managed to germinate, and it was heartbreaking. Luckily I fixed it with Duct tape and by burying the break under some soil, but I was very fortunate!

Usually you will put your seeds in a 5" or 7" pot as the pot is temporary until you plant it out. If you are growing the plant completely in your greenhouse, then put it in its final position now

Squash plants are very susceptible to frost damage because they have hollow stems (which is why they break so easily) which are very moist.

Even in your greenhouse if there is a risk of frost you should cover them with fleece to protect them.

Planting Our Squash Plants

Squash plants grow very rapidly and will quickly outgrow their pots. You should plant them out a couple of weeks after the last frost date, i.e. when the risk of frost has passed completely.

If you are planting them outside, then harden them off first or use cloches to protect them from the cold.

Squash plants appreciate a sheltered but sunny spot and will love a warm greenhouse! They are greedy plants and grow best when planted out into soil that has had plenty of compost of well-rotted manure dug in.

In you are growing in your greenhouse then allow plenty of space for them as they will grow to a massive size. Their leaves are huge and can grow to over two feet across. For most of us though these giant plants are just too big for a greenhouse and will need to be planted out.

Feeding and Watering
Squash plants are very greedy and thirsty plants, requiring a great deal of water as they grow. Once they have set fruit, they can require several gallons of water or more a day to maintain their growth. Irregular watering will cause the fruit to split and become stunted.

It is very important that you avoid getting water on the leaves of squash plants. They are very susceptible to powdery mildew, and if water sits on the leaves, it will encourage this fungal infection. In a greenhouse, water on the leaves can cause leaf burn which will damage your plant and in worst cases, kill it. Therefore, water at the base of the plant where the roots are carefully avoiding splashing water on the leaves.

Pests and Problems
Squashes are susceptible to powdery mildew, as we have just discussed, and a variety of other diseases. In most cases, you are not going to encounter any of them and are far more likely to have problems from pests.

Slugs and snails are probably your biggest enemy as they will happily devour your tender seedlings. They will also, rather surprisingly I think, chew their way through the actual pumpkins too!

I would recommend going on regular slug patrol and also using slug pellets or an alternative organic method of your choice (there are organic slug pellets on the market now).

The fruits themselves don't like to get wet, so if you damp down your greenhouse floor, you will need to lift your pumpkins off the ground either put them on pallets, wood, straw or something similar. Just be careful moving them as the stems have a habit of snapping.

You can learn more about growing squashes in my book on growing giant pumpkins, available in paperback and as a Kindle book from Amazon. This complete guide details everything from preparing the soil to getting the right seeds to germinating the seeds and caring for your pumpkins.

Squashes are worth starting off in your greenhouse, but unless you are in a very cold area, i.e. at the same latitude as Scotland or further north, they will grow outside. They will take up a lot of space in your greenhouse but if you can find a dwarf and smaller varieties they will fit better.

GROWING ZUCCHINI

Zucchini, or courgettes, in the UK, are a very easy vegetable to grow and will produce an abundance of fruit over the summer. Seriously, an abundance, I mean a single plant will produce so many that you will despair on what to do with them (try courgette chocolate cake, it's delicious)!

These plants grow very well in a greenhouse and can be left to mature in one. Alternatively, you can start them off as seedlings in your greenhouse and then plant them outside when the risk of frost has passed.

One of the nice things about zucchini plants is that there are so many different varieties on the market from green to yellow to round and more. My personal favorites are the yellow and round courgettes simply because I can buy a green one any day in the shop! Of course, there are a huge variety of green courgettes on the market and growing your own is a good opportunity to try a few varieties to see which you prefer.

Propagation

Seeds are sown between March and May, depending on where in the world you are. They are sown just like squashes, i.e. singularly in pots about 1cm under the soil on their sides. Remember to label your pots, particularly if you are growing a number of different varieties or other squash plants. They are very difficult to tell apart when they are small!

If you can, put a propagator lid on the pots, and within a week you will see the seedling pushing up from under the soil.

Once this happens, you can remove the propagator lid and move the pot to a sunny spot. If the seedling can get plenty of light, then it will grow very quickly.

Potting On Your Plants

Zucchini plants grow very quickly, and it won't be long before you need to pot them on. Carefully move them into a new, larger pot to allow them to keep growing.

You can feed your seedlings to give them an extra boost with a good liquid fertilizer. Some plants may need to be staked to prevent them from drooping.

Although the seedlings need regular watering, be careful not to over-water them.

Planting Out

If your greenhouse is a good size, then you can grow your zucchini plants to full size under glass. For most of us though we will grow them outside.

After the risk of frost has passed, you can plant the young plants outside, though keep an eye on the weather. If it feels like it may get cold, then you should fleece your plants or put cloches over them.

Remember to harden your plants off before you plant them out to reduce shock to them.

Zucchini plants like a sheltered but sunny position. They like to spread their roots so plant them in deep holes. When planting more than one plant, leave about two to three feet between plants as they will grow to a substantial size.

Watering and Feeding

Like other squashes, zucchini plants are greedy and thirsty. Also like other squashes, they do not appreciate water on their leaves and run the risk of developing powdery mildew.

Always water direct to the roots. Irregular watering can cause the fruits to split or drop.

Feed regularly with a good liquid fertilizer according to the instructions on the product.

Pests and Problems

There are a few diseases that affect zucchini plants but, like squashes, you are unlikely to encounter many of these.

Your biggest problem will be slugs and snails. They will devour young seedlings as well as the fruits. Take the usual precautions to prevent these pests destroying your harvest.

Harvesting

Zucchini plants are incredibly prolific and will produce a lot of fruits. You can pick them at any size from a few inches long; it depends on your personal preference. Be warned though they will appear to go from small, shop sized zucchini to giant barges literally overnight!

They produce so much fruit you will struggle to use it all with more than a couple of plants. Your friends and family though are likely to appreciate a gift of fresh zucchini!

Growing zucchini in your greenhouse is very easy to do. Unless you have a large greenhouse or live in a cold area, it is best to plant them outside because of their space requirements. They are very rewarding to grow and will produce a substantial crop for you to enjoy.

GROWING POTATOES

Potatoes are a very popular crop to grow at home. Most people are not going to grow potatoes in a greenhouse because they are a hardy vegetable and more than happy to grow outside in most climates.

If you live in a cold climate in an area with a short growing season, then you may have no choice but to grow them under glass.

Another reason to grow your potatoes in your greenhouse is if the area you live in is affected by potato blight. Plants growing in a greenhouse are much less susceptible to wind-borne diseases such as the dreaded blight.

When you grow potatoes in a greenhouse, you have to grow them in containers. You can buy potato bags to grow in, which are reusable. Alternatively, you can use normal pots, buckets, barrels or even compost bags. You can grow them in pretty much anything so long as there is sufficient drainage in the container.

You don't want to grow potatoes in the ground in a greenhouse. Most people don't grow directly in the ground in a greenhouse anyway, but if you do, then you want to avoid growing potatoes directly in the soil.

The reason is that no matter how thoroughly you dig the ground you will miss at least one potato and they will pop up the following year, and the year after, and keep on appearing! Also, potatoes are susceptible to diseases which build up in the soil, so if you are growing them in the ground, then you will struggle to rotate your crops to protect them from these diseases and pests.

For a container that is two feet tall and about 1½ feet wide, you can plant three seed potatoes. To plant five seed potatoes, you will need a container at least two feet wide and 2½ feet tall. Most potato grow bags will comfortably hold four or five potatoes.

There are a lot of different types of potatoes on the market which take different times to mature. First earlies are the quickest to mature but don't store as well as main crop potatoes, which take longer to mature.

Chit the potatoes before you plant them, i.e. leave them somewhere dark but warm to produce shoots. This is done as early as the end of January and start of February for first early potatoes. Once the shoots are about an inch long, you can plant them out. This will take approximately six to seven weeks.

When the potatoes start to produce shoots above the ground, they are frost tender and should be covered at the first sign of frost. Usually, though the risk of frost has passed by the time your potatoes are at this stage of growth.

The chitted potatoes are planted in their containers spaced approximately five inches apart and then covered with a few inches of compost. As the shoots appear above the soil, you earth them up which means you cover them with soil. Don't worry; it won't kill your plants, they will continue to grow. What it does is stop the potatoes going green, which they do when exposed to daylight, and then they become toxic.

Position the containers in your greenhouse where they will get a good amount of sun. They will need regular watering to produce a good crop but take care not to overwater them as that can cause the potatoes to rot.

As they are growing in containers, your potatoes will need regular feeding. Use a good quality liquid fertilizer and apply once or twice a week. Potatoes are greedy plants and will quickly exhaust the available nutrients in the compost.

Depending on the variety of potato you have planted they will be ready to be harvested anytime from June through to September. You can even buy late season potatoes which are designed to be planted in September for a Christmas harvest!

Potatoes can be stored in a paper or hessian sack in a cool dark place for quite some time. A main crop potato will store for up to six months whereas a first early potato will typically store for just a couple of months.

You can learn a lot more about growing potatoes both in the greenhouse and outside in my book "How to Grow Potatoes – The Guide to Choosing, Planting and Growing in Containers Or the Ground" available in paperback and Kindle on Amazon.

Potatoes are a fun crop to grow and are very rewarding. Kids in particularly love to grow them, and they are a staple crop for many of us. Unless you live in an area where blight is a major problem or the growing season is very short, you should grow them outside. Remember your greenhouse space is very valuable, and you want to grow the crops you cannot grow outside under your precious glass.

Growing Cucumbers

Cucumbers are another popular greenhouse plant. They love the warmth and have quite a long growing season, meaning they are difficult for many people to grow outside.

There are a lot of varieties of cucumbers from the normal ones you see in the stores to smaller, gherkin varieties, white varieties, and round varieties. Personally, I prefer to grow the more unusual varieties simply because I cannot buy them. I also think they taste a lot better too!

Propagation

Depending on the variety you are planting you will start them off any time from late March through to late May.

They are planted similarly to squashes, i.e. started off in individual pots with care to be taken to position the seed on its side. Cover it with about an inch of compost and water well.

The seed should germinate within anywhere from 4 to 14 days, depending on the variety you have planted.

When choosing your variety, you should check whether the plant is self-pollinating or not. There is a trend at the moment towards seeds that produce mainly female flowers, but not all of these are self-pollinating.

If you do buy a variety that isn't self-pollinating, then you will need more than one plant or to pollinate it by hand. Remember to allow plenty of pollinating insects into your greenhouse to help you out here too.

Once the plant has grown to a few inches high, you will want to pot it on to help it to continue to grow. Whether you move it to a larger pot or its final growing position is up to you and depends on the space available in your greenhouse.

Cucumber plants are very sensitive to cold weather and should be located in a sunny part of your greenhouse. If your greenhouse is unheated and the temperature looks like it will drop, then you should wrap them in fleece to protect them.

Cucumbers have shallow root systems and so do not need putting in massive pots. However, they do need regular watering because they dry out very quickly, which will damage the fruits.

Supporting Your Plants

Cucumbers grow into long, leggy plants and will creep all over your greenhouse. They need some support so that they grow upwards and take up less space. The major benefit of growing vertically is that the cucumbers are straighter and have some protection from slugs and snails. I have found that cucumbers grown vertically like this have softer, thinner skins too, which improves their flavor.

Use canes, trellises, netting or whatever you have to hand to support the plants. They will need you to help them to get started on their support, but they will quickly get the hang of it and grow upwards. Many people will train their cucumber plants to grow along the roof of their greenhouse, so the cucumbers hang down.

Watering and Feeding

Cucumbers have a high water content and to grow well need regular watering. If they are watered irregularly, then you can end up with stunted cucumbers or the skins will become tough and split.

Avoid over-watering your cucumber plants and make sure you water directly to the roots. Try to avoid getting water on the leaves as it can cause powdery mildew and leaf burn.

Give the plants a good soaking once a week and then regularly water the rest of the time. Because of their water needs, cucumber plants benefit a lot from a greenhouse irrigation system.

These plants appreciate their food and will benefit from a regular liquid feed. About four weeks after planting them out into their final position you need to start feeding them one a week. This will help keep the plant strong and allow it to develop plenty of healthy fruit.

Pests and Diseases

There are a number of diseases that affect cucumbers, but you are unlikely to see most of them when growing at home. Keep an eye on your plant and if the leaves look damaged then check for diseases. So long as you provide

70

good air circulation, you will avoid many possible diseases by growing your cucumbers in a greenhouse.

Most problems you will encounter are going to be pest related. Unfortunately, they are considered a tasty snack by many common pests.

Watch out in particular for slugs and snails. They are most likely to damage the cucumbers themselves rather than the leaves, but they will destroy seedlings. Keep an eye out for their trails and take the usual precautions to deal with these voracious pests.

Aphids are another common problem on cucumbers, and these can be removed by hand, sprayed off with water or taken care of with biological controls. A very dilute soap solution can be used but be careful as cucumbers are sensitive plants.

There are other pests you could encounter, but most of these come in on the wind and so are unlikely to make an appearance in your greenhouse. If you change the soil you are growing your cucumbers in every year; then you are highly unlikely to encounter any of these pests.

Harvesting

Most varieties of cucumbers will turn yellow when they are ripe, and at this point they are inedible. Cucumbers are picked while they are still green. Which size you pick them at will depend on the variety that you are growing.

As most cucumbers grow longer, they become tougher and less juicy. Keep removing the cucumbers to encourage the plant to produce more fruits.

Cucumbers are a great crop to grow in a greenhouse, and for many of us, that is our only option for successfully growing a good crop. Train the plant to grow up and over the roof of your greenhouse, and it will produce a great crop while not taking up too much space. Remember to water these delicate plants regularly, and you can enjoy a bountiful crop of cucumbers in the summer months.

GROWING GRAPE VINES

Grapes are considered an unusual crop for the home grower. These can be difficult to grow due to their sensitivity to the weather and long growing season.

There are a lot of different varieties on the market, and they all have slightly different requirements. Choose a variety that will suit your needs, i.e. certain varieties are better for eating than wine making and so on.

Grape vines grow to a massive size and so will need a lot of care and attention to stop them taking over your greenhouse. I inherited a 20-year-old grape vine in the greenhouse on my allotment, and it was a battle to even get inside the greenhouse because it had taken over!

Unless your greenhouse is bigger than 8x10' you should only grow a single grape vine. Any more and you will struggle to grow anything else under glass. One benefit of a grape in a greenhouse though is you can train it to grow along the roof and provide some shade for more delicate plants.

Preparation

Grapes grow best in a greenhouse when the vine is planted outside the greenhouse, and the growth is trained into the greenhouse through gaps at floor level. You can plant the vine directly into the soil in the border of the greenhouse, but you will have a lot more watering to do.

Before you plant the vine, dig over the soil and dig in some well-rotted manure and fertilizer. If the soil doesn't drain well, then put a thick layer of gravel at the bottom of the hole to prevent your plant getting waterlogged.

Propagation

Grape vines are rarely started from seed, purely down to the time it takes for them to mature and produce fruit.

They are usually bought as baby plants, typically one or two feet tall and then planted out. Depending on where you buy them from the young vines could be larger or smaller.

Make sure you buy a healthy vine and not one that looks unwell.

Planting

Your grape vine should be planted at one end of your greenhouse, opposite the door. It is then trained along the sides of the greenhouse, parallel to the roof ridge and towards the door.

Plant them out in November or December to the same depth they were in the original pot. Tease the roots out before you plant it. If necessary, prune the young vine to train it in the direction you want it to grow.

Feeding Your Grape Vine

Grapes like their food and so every spring, before the vine starts to grow, sprinkle the base of the vine with a good pelleted fertilizer and some dried blood. This gives it a good start when it comes out of its dormancy.

Throughout the growing season grapes will appreciate a further sprinkling of dried blood at a rate of about 30g per square meter or 1oz per square yard.

Every three weeks in the spring you need to feed your grape vine with a high potassium fertilizer, such as your regular tomato feed.

Once the leaves are fully set, then feed once a week.

As the grapes start to ripen and gain their color, stop feeding the grapevine as the tomato food can influence the taste of the grapes.

Watering Your Grape Vine

You should thoroughly water your grape vine every seven to ten days throughout the growing season.

Grape vines that have their roots inside a greenhouse will need watering more frequently than those with their roots outside. During a dry spell, the vines will need more frequent watering.

Where the roots are outside of the greenhouse, let the weather guide you as to how much you water your vine.

Mulching

Grape vines benefit from a good mulch in the spring with well-rotted manure. Apply this before the growth starts.

During the summer months, you can mulch the borders in your greenhouse with straw which helps keep the atmosphere dry. This helps both with pollination and with making the fruits set.

Caring for Your Grape Vine

Every three to four years your grape vine will benefit from you digging out a trench about 6 foot from the main stem, 2 foot wide and deep enough to reach the rubble you put in for drainage.

Remove this soil and use it elsewhere in your garden (but not for any grape vines) and replace it with fresh topsoil. This will help to prevent the build-up of pests and diseases in the soil.

Depending on your grape vine it may need some assistance with pollination. The best way to do this is to stroke your cupped hand over each of bunch of flowers to spread the pollen between them.

Your grape vine will produce tendrils, which are thin, twisty stems. These are used to support the growth of the vine but you will want to remove them. If you leave them on, then they get caught up in the grapes and get in the way of your pruning and training plan.

You can prune your vine back any time of the year, but the main pruning should be when the vine is dormant (late November and December). Here you can cut it back quite hard and train it to grow where you want it to go.

Pests and Problems

The most common problem you will encounter is powdery or downy mildew. This is typically brought on by poor ventilation and air circulation, i.e. your greenhouse is too full of plants! A good prune, cutting back some fresh growth and opening vents or windows can help to alleviate this problem.

Wasps can be an issue, particularly as the weather cools and they start hunting for sugary things, like ripe grapes. If they are an issue, then use wasp traps in your greenhouse.

Most other diseases won't affect your grape vine as it is in a greenhouse.

One thing to watch out for is a magnesium deficiency as this is common in grapes, but if you are feeding it regularly, this shouldn't be an issue.

Grape vines are good to grow in a greenhouse, and for many of us in the more northerly latitudes, it is the only way to grow grapes. They will take up a lot of space, so you need to be prepared to be quite harsh in your pruning, but if you do so then you can be rewarded with a healthy grapevine producing a good crop of fresh grapes!

GROWING TROPICAL PLANTS

Some people are interested in growing tropical plants in their greenhouse, particularly if they are in cooler areas.

Depending on the tropical plant this may, or may not, be possible. Some tropical plants are frost hardy or at the very least will tolerate cooler temperatures. However, others will die at the very thought of a chilly day.

Cacti in particularly are reasonably tolerant of cold weather though they won't appreciate being covered with a frost. Cacti will spend most of the year in your greenhouse but will appreciate fleecing in the winter to prevent the frost damaging them.

If you want to grow tropical plants then, realistically, you are going to have to heat your greenhouse and maintain a tropical temperature. This means it is going to be expensive!

Growing tropical plants will mean you need a specialist greenhouse as it needs to have excellent insulation to keep in the heat and the moisture. You will also need fans for air circulation and suitable ventilation too.

It isn't a cheap undertaking by any stretch of the imagination, but it can be done. What is important is to minimize heat loss from your greenhouse because that will reduce your heating costs. Tropical plants require a very specific environment and you may need to get some specialist advice on the environment they need.

Depending on the tropical plant it may need a high humidity level, which again means plenty of water. Most tropical plants will benefit from an irrigation system as some can be very sensitive to variations in watering. To maintain the right humidity may require specialist equipment.

Ultimately it depends on what you are planning to grow. There are so many potential plants you can grow that this is its own book and I won't cover it in depth here due to its specialized nature.

If you are planning on growing tropical plants, then I would strongly recommend you do a lot of research online first to understand the growing conditions of the plants you want to own.

You will then need to design your greenhouse around these plants and install all of the relevant equipment. It isn't a cheap undertaking, but it certainly can be done.

A properly tropical hothouse is a very specialist piece of equipment and will need under floor heating, along with many other specialist bits of equipment. Depending on what you are growing you may be able to get away with having it in your greenhouse in the summer and then moving it into your home in the winter.

PREPARING YOUR GREENHOUSE FOR SPRING

Once winter has passed work begins in earnest for the spring. This is probably one of the busiest times for a gardener, and there is lots of work to do. It is much easier to do this maintenance work before you fill your greenhouse with plants.

As winter draws to an end, you need to head out to your greenhouse and check it over. You are looking for any damage, cracked panes, missing clips and so on. Perform any necessary repairs on your greenhouse before spring comes.

Check all vents and windows to ensure they work properly and make sure all the glass is securely fitted in place.

Now is a good time to give the glass a good clean too. If you have plants overwintering in your greenhouse, then you need to be careful about using chemicals otherwise give it a good scrub to get rid of dirt and algae.

A wooden greenhouse can benefit from a coat of paint at the start of the year to preserve the wood and prevent any damage. Now is also the time to repair any damaged wood too.

The inside of your greenhouse needs clearing out too. Remove any rubbish, pull up weeds and give the floor a good sweep.

Look out for any pests that have spent the winter in your greenhouse such as slugs or snails. Remove them and re-introduce them to the great outdoors. In particular look out for any eggs or egg sacs and remove those too.

Check all your greenhouse equipment is working properly such as fans and heaters. Check your staging too and perform any required repairs.

Now is a good time to re-organize your greenhouse if you feel the need. You may have decided to change how things are laid out in your greenhouse after the last growing season. Before you fill the greenhouse with plants, you should move things around as it is much easier to do without pots all over the place.

For those who grow directly in the ground, you need to dig in compost or well-rotted manure to prepare the soil for planting. The greenhouse could benefit from the top few inches of soil being removed and used elsewhere in your garden to prevent the build-up of pests and diseases.

Otherwise, check your weed membrane, paving, and concrete to ensure it is secure and no weeds are growing through it. Depending on what you have for a greenhouse floor it could do with a good clean too which will remove pests, diseases, and algae.

It is worth checking you have enough pots and growing containers for what you are planning on growing. If you are re-using containers from the previous year, then they can benefit from a good wash using a dilute soap or bleach to kill any pests or diseases. Give them a good rinse afterward and leave them to dry. Remember that slugs and snails will hide in empty pots, so they are best stored somewhere other than your greenhouse.

Preparing for spring is all about getting ready for the growing season. This is where you plan what you are going to grow, decide where things will go in your greenhouse and generally warm up for the rush of planting that is to follow.

You prepare by making repairs to your greenhouse and buying any equipment you've decided you need for the next growing season. As you use your greenhouse, you will discover exactly what you need, and it is always worth getting it in before the growing season starts. If you are really lucky then maybe Santa Claus will bring you the items that you are missing for your greenhouse!

It is worth taking the time to perform these tasks because it will help extend the life of your greenhouse, ensure a healthy crop and prevent the build-up of pests and diseases in your greenhouse. It makes the growing season easier, allowing you to focus on planting rather than maintenance.

OVERWINTERING YOUR GREENHOUSE

Winter is a time when, although there may not be a lot growing, there is still work to be done in the greenhouse. Much of this work is simple to do, but it will help you get the most out of your greenhouse and keep you occupied.

Winter Jobs

Start by moving inside any plants that will not survive the winter outside.

More delicate plants can be wrapped in fleece or bubble wrap. Wrap it around the pot and then drape it over the plant itself, tying it loosely around the container so it forms a mini-greenhouse. Bubble wrap is best used directly on the pot, but fleece is better to put around the plant as it allows for air circulation and stops moisture building up around the plant.

Check all your heaters are working and that you have sufficient fuel (if required) for the winter. Make sure that the thermostats work properly so you don't have any nasty surprises.

Cut back any foliage that hangs over your greenhouse or blocks the light so that the plants in your greenhouse get plenty of light. This is surprisingly important as this extra light can make a big difference in keeping plants healthy and warm. It can also remove the risk of branches falling on your greenhouse in high winds and breaking the glass.

Winter Greenhouse Planting

There are a surprising amount of plants you can grow over winter, but most importantly towards the end of winter is when you start off many vegetables with long growing seasons.

Daffodils, hyacinth, crocus and other spring bulbs can be started off in your greenhouse over the winter months. When the hard frosts have passed, they can be planted out.

Towards the end of winter, you can start your brassicas, tomatoes, and aubergines (eggplants). These have a long growing season and starting them off early can ensure a successful crop. If you can start a few off every couple of weeks, then you will end up with an almost continuous crop over the summer.

Other winter vegetables include lettuce varieties such as Little Gem which needs lots of light but will grow in a greenhouse over winter. You may need to cover it with fleece on the colder days, but it will still produce a good crop.

Green leafy vegetables such as Pak Choi, cabbage, kale, and spinach are great to grow over winter. They tend to mature in the colder months and are particularly hardy. Other vegetables that will grow are radishes, carrots, turnips (rutabaga), and beetroot.

Of course, if you have a heated greenhouse then there is a lot more available to you to grow. For those without, you are more limited and will need to be on frost watch to fleece your plants and protect them from the cold.

If the temperature does get a bit warm over winter, then be prepared to open the vents. Just make sure they are closed mid-afternoon as some of the warmth of the day will be retained in the greenhouse. The air circulation will help keep your plants healthy.

Pests are unlikely to be a problem, but you may find some, particularly slugs and snails will get into your greenhouse to get out of the cold. Keep an eye on your plants for pest damage and take appropriate action.

Most plants will require less water over winter so be careful you do not overwater them. Too much water will kill your plants as surely as too little water.

There is a lot you can do in a greenhouse over winter. It does not need to be left empty, and even if you do not heat your greenhouse, there are still things you can grow and enjoy in these colder months.

POTENTIAL GREENHOUSE PROBLEMS

A greenhouse will have its own set of problems and if you have never grown in a greenhouse before it can be a little overwhelming and challenging. This section will detail some of the common greenhouse problems you will face and how to overcome them.

Damping Off

This is caused by soil-borne fungi and fungus-like organisms which infect your seedlings and causing them to decay and collapse, or "damp off."

This will, unfortunately, affect pretty much any seedling, particularly when the humidity levels are high, air circulation is poor or if the seeds are sown too thickly.

It is a common problem in greenhouses, more so when you use lidded propagators or otherwise cover your seedlings.

Damping off is a serious problem in spring when temperatures and light levels are lower. However, it can occur at any time of the year.

- The symptoms vary but include:
- The seedlings failing to emerge
- The seedlings collapse with a whitish fungal growth
- White fungus seen on the top of the soil

You can reduce the risk of this disease by using a good quality seed compost. Check it is sterile as it will be free from pathogens. Home-made compost could well contain the fungi that cause this disease, particularly if you have composted diseased soil.

Using new pots and growing trays can help eliminate the risk of this disease. If you are reusing pots from the previous year, then they should be thoroughly cleaned first. Also, treat them with a disinfectant to kill off any pathogens.

If you do get damping off disease in any pots, then get rid of the pots. Do not use them again.

The main cause of damping off is poor air circulation between seedlings. If you sow your seeds thinly and avoid overcrowding, it will help reduce the risk of this disease.

If you are collecting rainwater for use on your seedlings, then cover your water butt to prevent the pathogens entering your water.

It is better to use mains water as that will be clean with no risk of introducing damping off disease to your seedlings.

Keep the seedlings well ventilated. If you are growing in plastic propagators, then remove the lids during the day and when the seedlings have made an appearance above the soil.

Avoid overwatering your seedlings as damping off disease loves a warm, damp environment.

Regularly cleaning both your greenhouse and your water butt will prevent the pathogen that causes damping off disease.

There are currently no chemical controls for damping off disease.

Grey Mold

Botrytis Cinerea causes this disease and normally gets into your plants through a wound or infects them while they are stressed. However, healthy plants can contract this disease in humid conditions. Grey mold can appear any time during the year.

This disease is most common in grapes, beans, cucumbers, zucchinis, tomatoes and lettuces in a greenhouse though will occur on some other crops outside of a greenhouse.

It is particularly a problem for plants grown in a humid or overcrowded greenhouse.

This is noticeable by a fuzzy gray mold growing on infected leaves, buds, fruit or flowers. When the humidity is low, the infections may stay in small areas, but in a higher humidity environment, the disease will spread quickly.

In infected material, you will see small black, seed-like formations. Flowers and buds will shrivel up and die. The fruit, particularly on grapes, will turn to soft brown rot.

Removing dead and dying plant material will help reduce the risk of this disease.

Improving ventilation will reduce humidity and therefore the risk of this disease. Avoiding overcrowding your plants will allow for better air circulation which also reduces the risk of this disease.

There are currently no fungicides available to combat gray mold.

Glasshouse Red Spider Mite

This is probably one of the most irritating pests in a greenhouse and is a sap sucking mite that attacks the leaves of your plants. The leaves become mottled in appearance and in severe infestations your plants will lose leaves and even die.

These mites aren't too fussy about what they attack and are common in grapes, eggplant (aubergine), tomatoes, peppers, orchids, cucumbers, peaches and more. There are few plants that this pest won't attack!

These pests love warm, dry conditions, such as those found in a greenhouse. Usually, they are only active from around March to October, but if you heat your greenhouse, they can be a problem all year round.

On the upper leaf surface, you will see a pale mottling if your plant is infected. On the underside of the leaf you can see tiny, yellowish-green mites and egg shells. As these are quite small, you may need a magnifying glass to see them.

In the most severe infestations, you can see a fine silk webbing on your plants. Also, the leaves lose their green color, dry up and even fall off. In the worst infestations, the plants become so weak, they die.

Glasshouse red spider mite is quite hard to control because it breeds so quickly. Certain strains of the mite are resistant to some pesticides too.

A biological control is a good idea as it means using fewer chemicals and risking further damage to delicate plants. The predatory mite *Phytoseiuus Persimilis* is the most commonly used biological control for this pest. Be aware though that this predator is susceptible to the same pesticides you would use against red spider mites.

The worst affected plants will need removing from greenhouse towards the end of summer. The lower temperatures make the female mites seek somewhere to overwinter. Taking them out of your greenhouse means the pest doesn't overwinter inside.

Clear your greenhouse of all debris, pots and everything else and wash the greenhouse down thoroughly. Keep weeds in and around your greenhouse down to a minimum as these mites can hide in them.

Ensuring your greenhouse isn't overcrowded will help reduce not only the risk of infection but the speed with which it spreads.

There are pesticides on the market which will tackle this pest but you need to read the label very carefully. Some of them are not suitable for edible plants. You shouldn't spray any plant in flower as the pesticide will kill friendly, pollinating insects.

On edible plants, you can use plant extracts, oils or fatty acids. Make sure you read the label and apply any pesticide according to recommended instructions.

Glasshouse Leafhopper

This is a small, sap-sucking insect which causes a pale mottling on the upper leaf surface of plants in a greenhouse.

In the worst infestations, the spots end up joining together giving the leaves the appearance of a mineral deficiency.

Once treated, infected leaves will remain discolored, but new growth will be normal.

Adult leafhoppers are quite small, about 1/8" (3mm) long. They are a pale yellow color with gray markings, being widest at the head end and tapering to a point. When disturbed they hop off the leaves and fly short distances.

The nymphs are easier to spot as they are creamy white, wingless and much less active.

Unfortunately, there is no way of controlling this pest without using chemicals.

When you spot these pests, you should spray with an appropriate pesticide. Remember to read the label carefully as not all pesticides are suitable for edible crops.

Pesticides containing pyrethrum are effective and considered organic. Pesticides containing acetamiprid and cypermethrin are also effective, but these ingredients are not suitable for edible crops. Remember, don't spray plants in flower as you will end up killing pollinating insects.

Glasshouse Whitefly

This is another sap-sucking pest which will literally suck the life out of your plants! They excrete a sugary substance called honeydew onto your plants. This allows for the growth of black, sooty molds.

Pretty much any plant is fair game for whitefly, whether it is ornamental or vegetable.

Glasshouse whitefly loves warm conditions and can be active throughout the year in your greenhouse.

This pest is very easy to spot because when you disturb an infected plant a cloud of these small, white winged insects will fly up into the air. You can usually spot the nymphs on the bottom of the leaves too.

This pest reproduces very rapidly and has developed some pesticide resistant strains. Biological controls are considered to be the most effective way of dealing with this pest.

The parasitic wasp, *Encarsia Formosa* preys on the whitefly nymphs and is available to buy online. This predator should be introduced into your greenhouse before the infestation gets out of control as it does not provide an instant solution. This predatory wasp though is killed by most pesticides so be careful about using any sprays in your greenhouse.

You can get sticky yellow sheets to hang around infected plants which catch adult whitefly.

Whiteflies will also infect weeds so keeping the weeds down helps to control this pest.

The main way whitefly is brought into a greenhouse is through the introduction of new plants. It is worth checking new plants for signs of whitefly or even quarantining them before bringing them into your greenhouse.

There are numerous insecticides you can use but remember to check that they are suitable for the types of plants you are growing. Some whitefly have developed resistance to certain pesticides so if one doesn't work, buy another with a different main ingredient.

Aphids

Aphids are another sap-sucking bug that is smaller than ¼". Some aphid varieties are known as greenfly or blackfly though there are plenty of other types out there, including wooly aphids which mainly attack trees.

Aphids feed on your plants and are usually found on new growth. Ants often farm them and sometimes the ants are the first indication you get of this pest. Check new growth and the underside of young leaves to see if your plants are infected.

They are easily spotted, but you can often see their effect where young leaves are curled or otherwise distorted. Virtually no plant is safe from them as there are hundreds of different types of aphid.

Aphids though are a tasty snack for a wide variety of predatory insects such as ladybirds, hoverfly larvae and a variety of parasitic wasps. There are biological controls available to control aphids.

In less serious infestations you can just squash the aphids by hand.

There are a lot of insecticides on the market as aphids are a very common pest. You will need to spray the plant thoroughly, including the undersides of the leaves. Check that any insecticide you use is suitable for the type of plants you are growing.

Powdery Mildew

This is a real problem if you contract it, and is a fungal disease that mainly affects the foliage of your plants. In some cases, it will spread to the stems, and in rare cases it will infect both the flowers and the fruit.

A wide variety of plants are susceptible to powdery mildew though there are many different types of this fungus, each type infecting just a few different plants. Both ornamental and vegetable plants can contract powdery mildew.

There are a number of symptoms of powdery mildew, though the most obvious is the powdery patches of the fungus on your plant. In early stages, there is virtually no indication of the disease, and it is only spotted as it develops and the mildew starts to show.

All infected material must be destroyed. Giving your greenhouse a thorough clean and disinfect over winter will kill off any dormant spores and hopefully prevent a reoccurrence the following year.

Regular watering and a good mulch will help keep the plants strong, stopping them from suffering from water stress, so they are less prone to infection. Pruning any infected shoots as soon as you see them will also help to reduce the spread of the infection.

If this disease is a major problem for you, then you can buy a few varieties of plant which have some resistance to this fungus. Be aware that this fungus will infect some wild plants and spread to your greenhouse plants through them.

As this fungus grows on the surface of the leaf, it is ideally suited for treating with a spray. However, there are no sprays available which can be used safely on edible crops. There are some sprays which can be used on ornamental plants but make sure you read you label carefully.

Some people claim a milk spray can cure powdery mildew, though having tried it outdoors on pumpkins I've yet to see its effectiveness.

Avoiding water sitting on leaves overnight and making sure there is sufficient air circulation and ventilation will help reduce the risk of this disease.

POLLINATION IN A GREENHOUSE

Pollination is, as I am sure you know, vital if you want your plants to produce fruit. It can be difficult to get your plants pollinated in a greenhouse as it is a closed system.

Pollinating insects need access to your flowers to perform their job. This means you need to ensure vents and windows are open when the flowers are open. This will allow these beneficial insects access so they can perform pollination duties.

Leaving your greenhouse door open when you can help to encourage pollinators inside. Of course, depending on where your greenhouse is located this may only be possible when you are there.

You can deliberately introduce pollinators into your greenhouse, though you need to ensure there is sufficient food for them to stay inside.

The alternative is to pollinate your plants by hand. Yes, you read that correctly and it surprisingly easy to do!

Male flowers usually have a single stamen in while female flowers often have a cluster. Pollen needs to be transferred between the flowers for pollination to take place.

The picture above shows you a female flower. You can clearly see the cluster of the stamen in the middle.

Above you can see a male flower. This has just a single stamen and is very different from the female flower.

Although you can do this by hand, it is far too easy to damage your plants as the flowers are very delicate. Brush the tip of your finger on a stamen until it has yellow pollen on it and then brush it on another flower.

Most people will do this either with cotton buds or a small paintbrush as they are the easiest ways to pollinate your plants. The same principle applies, get pollen on the object and then transfer it to the other flowers. As my allotment isn't close to home, I will often use pretty much anything to hand including tissues!

In the above picture, I have taken the pollen from a male flower and am brushing it against a female flower. You can clearly see the yellow pollen on the piece of tissue. A paint brush is a much better tool to use, but unfortunately, this was all I had to hand. Take the pollen from multiple male flowers of the same plant variety. If you are pollinating multiple varieties of plant, then use a different paint brush for each variety otherwise you could end up cross breeding your plants.

It is a delicate and time-consuming job but necessary if you want to ensure your plants produce a good crop of fruit. It is also important if you are trying to cross breed plants or pollinate specific varieties.

In most cases your plants will be pollinated naturally but if you find you are getting lots of flowers but no fruit it is down to a lack of pollination and you will have to give nature a helping hand.

PORTABLE GREENHOUSES

A full-size greenhouse is wonderful, but not everyone has the space or money for one. If you don't, then there are alternatives that will give you many of the benefits without the expense.

The above picture shows you my portable greenhouse which I bought reduced at the end of the growing season. It has given me a few years' service and is ideal for starting off seeds close to my back door, so they are easy to tend.

Portable greenhouses are much smaller and more fragile, but if you don't have enough space for a full-size greenhouse, then these are worth getting. You may only be able to get a few tomato and pepper plants in it, but it is more than you would otherwise have been able to grow!

Yes, I've squeezed rather a lot into that small greenhouse, but I got a decent crop. Plants were taken out during the day and warm weather and then put back in overnight to minimize the risk of disease and help air circulation. I got a great crop!

One advantage of these smaller greenhouses is that they allow you to, at the very least, start your seeds off early and protect them from unexpected frosts.

Portable plastic greenhouses come in all shapes and sizes suitable for a wide range of budgets. As these tend to come in large boxes, they are usually heavily discounted at the end of the growing season because the retailer doesn't want to take up precious storage space which could be used for more lucrative Christmas stock. Perfect for you to buy for the following year!

When I had a small concrete yard rather than a garden I bought a 4-foot wide and 3-foot deep portable, plastic greenhouse that stood about 7 feet tall. As there was no soil, this was all I had to grow in, so it got filled with tomato and pepper plants which grew remarkably well. Eventually, I was assigned an allotment to grow vegetables on, and then I kept the plastic greenhouse at home to start my seeds off. New seeds need a lot of attention, so it was much easier to have them close to hand rather than having to drive to my allotment.

These greenhouses come in a huge variety of shapes and sizes, so you will be able to find something suitable for the space you have in mind for it. Even if you have a greenhouse and a garden they can be useful as extra space or to start seeds off nearer to your door.

One word of caution though, these are much more fragile than traditional greenhouses and will need securing to the ground. I put grow bags on the bottom metal poles to provide weight so that it couldn't blow away. You should also use guy ropes if possible and position your portable greenhouse in a sheltered location.

Like normal greenhouses, these will get very hot and suffer from many of the same problems with overcrowding and poor air circulation. I would recommend that on warmer days you leave the door open.

The plastic covers can tear, but replacements are available, often from the original store you bought your portable greenhouse from or online.

A low to the ground, portable greenhouse can be used as a cold frame. These are great to have as well as a normal greenhouse because you can use them to help harden off your seedlings before planting them out.

Some people will recommend you avoid these plastic greenhouses as they only last a season but, in my experience, if they are looked after properly and located well they will last several years. The one I am currently growing in has been in use for three years and has still got a couple of years of service left in it.

The more expensive plastic greenhouses tend to have thicker plastic covers. These heavy duty covers will last a few more years as they are harder to damage. When exposed to UV light plastic has a tendency to become brittle and break, but if you buy a cover with UV protection, then it will last a little longer.

I would recommend that you take the portable greenhouse down when winter approaches. Snow, frost and high winds can damage the greenhouse and shorten its lifespan. As these greenhouses can be put up in 10 to 20 minutes, this isn't a great hardship.

Although these are good, they are no replacement for a proper glass greenhouse. However, they are better than nothing and worth owning until you do get a glass greenhouse. They are also handy companions to a glass greenhouse for when you run out of space and need somewhere for all those extra plants you've grown!

COLD FRAMES

Cold frames are a very useful accompaniment to a greenhouse. At one time these were found in every garden attached to the greenhouse but now have become free standing structures. These are used as mini greenhouses to start off seeds and harden off plants. Although they have declined in popularity somewhat due to the cheap availability of glass greenhouses they are still handy to have in your garden.

The cold frame provides a sheltered, warm environment where you can germinate seeds and start your seedlings off. As it is sheltered, a cold frame is ideal for growing plants such as cucumbers. These tend to be fairly low to the ground, so they aren't suitable for larger plants such as tomatoes.

For hardening off your plants, a cold frame is ideal. You move the plant to the cold frame, leaving the lid open for longer and longer until the plants get acclimatized to the weather.

Cold frames come in all shapes and sizes, and as the gardener often builds them, they are often unique in their design. You can purchase cold frames online and from gardening stores where they can cost anything from tens of dollars upwards.

Of course, if you don't want to buy one you can make your own cold frame, which many people do. You can recycle old windows, bricks, and wood to make a cold frame that fits the space you have in mind for it.

The traditional cold frame was a brick-walled cold frame, usually attached to the sunny side of the greenhouse (which would have been several layers of brick with the greenhouse on top). These would have varied in size with some being tall enough to stand in.

Larger brick cold frames were used as hotbeds, filled with rotting manure so the heat would warm the plants inside.

These are still popular with gardeners because they are easy to build from reclaimed bricks but nowadays tend to be free standing.

A wooden sided cold frame is very easy to build and can either be a wooden frame with glass in or solid wooden sides. Almost anyone will be able to build one of these, and if you have solid wooden sides, then this will help retain warmth, particularly if you insulate the wood with bubble wrap or something similar.

You can buy wooden sided cold frames though like wooden greenhouses they tend to be a little bit more expensive.

A cheaper option if you are buying a cold frame is one made of aluminum and glass. The glass sides let more light in which helps prevent the plants from becoming too leggy. However, the downside is that they do not retain heat, as well as a wooden or brick, sided cold frame. Also being glass, you have the same set of problems as you do with a glass greenhouse.

You can buy plastic cold frames which are twin walled, so they retain heat better. While they do not let in as much light, they protect your plants better from the cold.

One thing to be careful of with a wooden framed cold frame is that the wood can warp in hot, cold and wet weather. Make sure you treat the wood every year to protect it.

If you use raised beds, then these are very easy for you to convert to a cold frame. You can build a roof over the top of it. However, you need to be careful to ensure there is sufficient air circulation as it the seal is too good then it will encourage fungal growth.

There are plenty of woodworking plans available online for making your own cold frame, but at the end of the day, you can make something that suits your needs and the space you have for it. Your cold frame needs to be located somewhere that gets plenty of sunlight, particularly during the spring months. It needs to be easy to open and of a sufficient size for what you want to put in it.

Whether you decide to buy one or build your own is entirely up to you. However, a cold frame is a very useful addition to a greenhouse, being helpful in hardening off seedlings and giving you some extra space to grow tender plants.

Pit Greenhouses Explained

A pit greenhouse, or underground greenhouse, is a subject all of its one, one that could have an entire book written about it. It is an interesting variation on the greenhouse and is very useful in colder areas with heavy ground frosts.

For people who live in colder areas, a pit greenhouse will extend the growing season significantly and help you grow plants that you would otherwise be unable to grow due to the cold weather.

These are popular in the mountains of South America, Tibet, Japan, Mongolia as well as the Northern United States and Canada.

Pit greenhouses are sometimes referred to as walipini and use the heat of the sun and the insulation of the surrounding earth to warm the area you grow in. They are simple to build, cheap and very effective.

Typically, you will build a bit greenhouse into a natural slope, so very little of it is exposed to the cold. They are usually built of clay, stone or brick and are between 6 and 8 feet deep.

Usually, these are walk-in structures, and they can be heated if you prefer with electric or paraffin heaters. Without heating, they can keep the temperature a good 20F warmer than outside.

You will position your pit greenhouse, so it is south facing to maximize the amount of sun it gets, particularly on shorter days. The roof is commonly angled to let in as much light as possible.

When building a pit greenhouse, you need to ensure it is above the water table. If not, then you are going to find your greenhouse regularly flooded. You need the bottom of your pit greenhouse to be at least five feet above the water table.

The pit is marked out and dug, then lined with insulating material and construction material, e.g. brick. You may, depending on how cold it is where you live, build a double wall with insulating material in between the layers of brick.

One construction material that is used is bags of earth. These are the bags used in sandbags but filled with the earth excavated from the pit. These can be used internally as insulation and to build up the second wall.

The roof is then built up, so it is slanted at an angle. Again, good quality material is best to ensure it provides sufficient insulation. If you can build in some windows that open, then you will be able to provide ventilation in the summer months. As you know, this is vital to prevent fungal infections and other problems.

In extremely cold weather, the roof can be covered with further insulating material to prevent heat loss.

If your area suffers from heavy snowfall then you need to ensure that the roof angle is sufficient to prevent snow settling on the roof. The weight of the snow could end up damaging or even breaking your roof.

These are often built with the help of the local community and where they are used make a real difference in the accessibility of affordable fresh vegetables. Although you cannot grow as much in an unheated pit greenhouse as you could in a glass greenhouse further south you can grow a good variety of shorter season plants that would otherwise not grow.

Combine a pit greenhouse with vertical gardening, i.e. growing smaller plants such as lettuces in vertical racks, allows you to grow a lot of vegetables in a small area.

For those people living in colder areas with limited growing seasons, these are a great way to harness natural resources to allow you to grow fresh vegetables.

GROWING ALL YEAR ROUND

Greenhouses are great for your summer crops and extending your growing season, but if they are heated, you can grow all year long. However, this isn't particularly cost effective as the cost of heating your greenhouse far outweighs the cost of buying the vegetables you can grow.

Saying that though, even an unheated greenhouse helps you to grow throughout the year and can be very cost effective indeed.

In late winter and early spring, you can start off hardy plants such as cabbage, leeks, lettuce, peas, onions, broad beans, Brussels sprouts and so on. These are then planted out once the weather warms up.

If you do heat your greenhouse, then plants such as tomatoes and peppers can be started off early too.

In mid-spring, your more tender plants are started off, such as pumpkins, zucchini (courgettes), squashes, sweetcorn, French beans and so on. This means that towards late spring they are ready to be planted outside or under glass. At this time of year, you can also buy ready grown pepper and tomato plants for your unheated greenhouse.

As spring progresses and summer begins you can plant your summer plants in their final locations in your greenhouse. Your outdoor crops are hardened off and planted out once the risk of frost has passed, which frees up space in your greenhouse.

If you have space in your greenhouse then towards the end of summer you can sow lettuces, salad leaves, and even baby carrots under glass for a later crop. You can also plant your Christmas potatoes in bags.

In winter time you can sow your broad beans and peas to overwinter before being planted out in spring. Calabrese and French beans can be planted and will mature in the greenhouse. Hardy lettuces will also grow happily in your greenhouse. You can also start any over-winter onions too.

Hardy plants such as kale and chard typically grow well outside during the colder months, but in some areas, they may benefit from being under glass during the extreme cold to ensure you get a good crop.

What you can grow throughout the year in your greenhouse will depend greatly on where in the world you live and how cold it gets. In colder areas with heavy snowfall plants which would be left outside over winter (kale, Brussels sprouts, etc.) will benefit from the protection of the greenhouse. If nothing else this will prevent the snow from damaging the plants.

In warmer areas, the greenhouse will let you start your plants off much earlier so you can make the most of the growing season.

Unless you are going to heat your greenhouse, you will not be able to get crops such as tomatoes, cucumbers, peppers and chilies during the winter months. Unfortunately, the cost of heating tends to be prohibitive.

Most greenhouse owners will usually only heat their greenhouse enough to prevent frost, which will damage their tender plants. If you grow rare or unusual plants that cannot tolerate colder temperatures, then heating becomes much more expensive but necessary.

The location of your greenhouse plays a big part in how much you need to heat your greenhouse and what you can grow over the winter months.

A greenhouse positioned in a sunny, sheltered area will obviously remain warmer than one, such as mine, which is located in the open. A lean to greenhouse will be warmer because it benefits from the heat coming through the wall from the house behind.

When it comes to growing all year long, you can be creative. But with so many variables there are no hard and fast rules, so you will have to experiment, seeing what works best in your greenhouse in your area.

CLEANING YOUR GREENHOUSE

Greenhouse cleanliness is absolutely vital. Whether you own a greenhouse, a polytunnel, a cold frame or a portable greenhouse, regular cleaning is vital.

Over time pathogens such as bacteria, pests and fungus will build up in your greenhouse, and these can have a devastating effect on your plants.

When you clean your greenhouse will depend on what you grow in it. If you are only growing plants in the summer months, then you clean your greenhouse in winter, when the crops have all been cleared out.

However, if you grow all year round, then a mild spell in late September or October is the best time to clean. This allows you to put your delicate plants outside while you clean your greenhouse thoroughly. The cleaning also makes sure that your plants get maximum light during the darker winter months.

You will want to put aside a day to clean your greenhouse to ensure you have plenty of time to do the job. Choose a day that is dry and mild, particularly if you are putting tender plants outside.

Firstly, you need to remove your plants from the greenhouse. If you are concerned about them, then cover them with some horticultural fleece to keep them warm.

Then remove any empty pots, the greenhouse staging and as much as you can so the greenhouse is empty.

Your first job is to brush out all the debris from the greenhouse such as soil, fallen leaves and other odds and ends that have been dropped in the growing season. If you have a portable vacuum cleaner, then these are a big timesaver.

Any fallen leaves, particularly from tomatoes and squashes should be destroyed rather than composted.

The internal structure of the greenhouse then needs to be cleaned. Use hot water if you can and try to avoid chemicals which could remain in your greenhouse and harm your plants the following year.

Hydrogen peroxide is a particularly good cleaner that has little impact on the environment. There are specialist greenhouse cleaners on the market and garden disinfectants can be used.

You can use domestic cleaning products, but you need to be careful as these can contain harmful chemicals which can hang around in your greenhouse for months.

Once the structure is clean, then the panes need cleaning. Remove any old shade paint and give them a good scrub both inside and out. Remove any dirt trapped between the panes and, if necessary, remove panes to clean any algae.

Take this time to check the rubber seals and the glass clips on your greenhouse. Any that are perished, broken or missing need to be replaced. Also check all vents, vent controllers, and draught excluders, making good any necessary repairs.

The gutters on your greenhouse need to be cleaned out. Check the downpipes for blockages and remove any debris. Where the gutter meets the downpipe, there should be a wire mesh to prevent debris blocking the pipe. Make sure this is fixed in place properly, though if it is missing you need to buy or make one.

Check that all the gutters are firmly in place and are not leaning as this can lose you precious water.

Over summer your water butts will often gather debris and grow algae or harbor mosquito larvae. Empty out your water butts and give them a good scrub out using non-toxic cleaning products. Rinse the water butt thoroughly before putting back in position. You can add potassium permanganate crystals which turn the water a light pink color. This will help prevent the build-up of algae in the water.

Clean and replace the lids of your water butts as this helps prevent debris from getting into them.

Although dirty water won't harm your grown plants, it can be too much for delicate seedlings and seeds. It can contain pathogens that will harm them so always use tap or municipal water on your delicate plants.

If your greenhouse has a wooden frame, then you need to treat the wood as well. This will prevent the wood from rotting and extend the lifespan of your greenhouse.

Your greenhouse staging should also be cleaned like the rest of your greenhouse. If it is wooden, then treat it with an appropriate preservative to prevent rot or damage to it.

Any pots that are going to be reused should be emptied of compost and cleaned with a good disinfectant. This will prevent the build-up of bacteria and pests.

Once everything is cleaned and treated, then you can put everything back into your greenhouse. Take the opportunity to organize everything to make the best use of space and minimize the potential hiding places for pests looking to overwinter somewhere warm.

Giving your greenhouse a thorough cleaning once a year helps to keep pest and disease problems to a minimum. Think of it along the same principles as rotating your crops. You are preventing the build-up of potentially harmful pests and diseases. Don't avoid this job, make sure you do it as it will help to minimize problems the following growing season.

GREENHOUSE WEED CONTROL

Weeds are always a problem for the gardener, and the greenhouse gardener is no exception.

If you have built the foundation for your greenhouse properly, you should minimize the weeds coming up from under the ground. However, they are persistent and some, such as mares tail, dandelion, and dock, will persist.

Those who are growing direct in the soil will find weeds to be a constant problem, which is one reason why many greenhouse owners grow in containers. If you do grow in the soil, then regular weeding is the only real method to keep weeds down.

You can cover the soil with a high-quality weed membrane, cutting holes in it where you are putting plants. This is a good way to keep the weeds down and reduce the amount of work you need to do.

Containers should have no, or at least very few weeds. If you do see any, then remove them as soon as they appear and discard them.

You will see weeds growing in from outside your greenhouse or in any piles of dirt dropped on the floor. Keep your greenhouse clean to prevent weeds building up in discarded soil.

You must keep the soil surrounding your greenhouse weed free too. A lot of people will extend their greenhouse base a foot or so beyond the edge of their greenhouse purely to prevent weeds growing and invading the greenhouse.

Using Chemicals
You need to be very careful using any chemicals in your greenhouse. Many weed killers do not distinguish between a weed and a vegetable plant. They will kill vegetable matter indiscriminately.

The other issue you may face is that repeated use of chemicals will result in those chemicals building up in your greenhouse environment. Yearly cleaning of your greenhouse will help to prevent this from happening, but you still need to be aware of what you are using.

Even if you spray chemicals carefully, there is still a good chance that other plants will harmed so it is best not to use any chemicals if you can help it.

Organic sprays are effective, but many of those can still harm your vegetable plants.

Your best bet is to work to minimize the incidence of weeds in your greenhouse. If you have built your greenhouse properly, then there should be virtually no weeds coming up from under your greenhouse.

Making sure your greenhouse is weed free means there are fewer places for potential pests to hide. It also means the weeds are not competing with your plants for resources, giving your vegetable plants more of a chance to grow.

Set up your greenhouse to be as low maintenance as you can. Make sure there are no opportunities for weeds to get a footing and tackle any weeds as soon as you see them. Removing weeds when they are young prevents them from establishing root systems which can quickly spread.

Ideally weeding your greenhouse should be very little work at all. If you have set it up properly and keep your greenhouse tidy, then there should be very little for you to weed. However, keep a close eye on your greenhouse because weeds take resources from your vegetables and can encourage pests and diseases to take hold.

HOOP HOUSES & POLY TUNNELS

Hoop houses are a very easy and cheap greenhouse that you can build at home. Some people call these polytunnels which are essentially the same thing.

Having a hoop house is like moving your growing area several hundred miles south, allowing you to extend your growing season and grow plants that you would otherwise be unable to grow to maturity in your area.

Compared to glass greenhouses these are very low tech, but they are cheaper to construct. Obviously, the protection from frost is a huge benefit but so is the protection from the wind and the increased CO_2 levels in the tunnel.

For gardeners in more northerly areas, these are a real benefit for extending the growing season at a lower cost than a greenhouse.

Some hoop houses will come with roll up sides which helps with the all-important ventilation. Others will need shade cloth, but the extra warmth of a hoop house provides a very cheap way to cover a large area.

As these are reasonably fragile structures, being made of a thick plastic sheet over plastic tubing, it is wise to remove the plastic cover over winter to prevent damage from heavy rain or snowfall. If you don't live in an area that suffers from heavy snow during winter, then a hoop house can be strong enough to survive the winter intact.

Before you start building a poly tunnel or hoop house you need to think about the area you are going to cover. The size you need to build will influence the materials and construction method. Bigger hoop houses need stronger poles and covers and should be well staked down to prevent wind damage.

Think about whether you want your hoop house to be big enough for you to walk into or more. Some are 8 to 10 feet tall with grape vines trained along the roof! Do you also want roll up sides or other ventilation options?

If you are building your own, then you can design it specifically for your needs. However, you can buy pre-made poly tunnels that just need to be assembled. These aren't as expensive as you may think.

Location and Orientation

Like a greenhouse, a hoop house needs a flat site to be erected on. This should be an area that does not flood and ideally sheltered from the wind as these plastic tunnels are more easily damaged in high winds.

For maximum ventilation align the ends of your polytunnel with the prevailing winds. You want a good, deep soil so that you anchor it securely to the ground.

Building Your Own Polytunnel

Using PVC plastic pipes arches over a wooden frame on the ground and covered in a good, thick polyethylene plastic will create a hoop house up to 18 feet wide! Of course, you can make them smaller if you want.

Using 1½" diameter PVC pipes will work very well, though larger diameter pipes can provide a stronger framework. Galvanized steel pipe used in chain link fences works well for a frame because it is so sturdy. You will need a specialist pipe bending tool and the steel is more expensive. However, in an area susceptible to high winds and heavy snow this can make for a much stronger frame.

Step 1 – Build a Ground Frame

Firstly, you need to build a ground frame out of good quality rot-resistant timber. For a tunnel that is between 14 and 18 feet wide use 2x6 wood on its edge but for smaller hoop houses, you should use 2x4.

If the length of your tunnel is longer than the lumber, you have to use two-foot battens to splice the joints. Use 3" wood screws (No. 10) for the spliced joints and No. 10 4" screws for the corners.

Make sure the frame is square. Drive stakes into the corners as a temporary measure to keep the frame square while you build your polytunnel. These can be removed at a later stage.

Step 2 – Drive Ground Pipes

These are driven into the ground to maintain the rigidity of the frame and to support the PVC pipes that form the hoops.

You will want pipes between 18" and 36" in length (shorter for harder ground).

Use a sledgehammer to drive this into the ground, one at each corner and then another every 3 feet along the long sides. These are positioned on the inside face of the ground frame and opposite each other. They are driven into the ground until they are flush with the top of the ground frame.

If the ground is particularly hard, then give it a good soaking first which will help you get the pipes in without too much effort.

Step 3 – Positioning the Hoop Pipes

The length of PVC pipe required will depend on how wide your hoop house is and how high you want it. For an 18' wide house you will need two 10' and one 20' length of piping. Just make sure that when you buy the pipe, you get ones that are factory flared at one end; making it much easier to get the pipes together. One straight end slips into the flared end and then is glued together for additional support using a PVC cement.

As well as pipes forming the arch, you will need purlins, which are horizontal pipes running along the roof and either side of the roof to provide rigidity and support.

The hoops are then put into the ground pipes, which you may need some help doing. Once they are in place, you drill a hole through both the hoop and the ground pipe for a ¼" locking bolt. Use a 4" long carriage bolt. Just do one side for now and make sure the hoop is fully inserted into the ground pipe.

Next, you need to climb a stepladder and check the alignment of the roof. Adjust the hoop house as appropriate so that the peaks are all roughly the same height. Have a helper adjust the unbolted bottoms of the hoops until everything is the right height.

Once the roof is properly aligned, drill and bolt the ends of the hoops into the ground pipes, taking care not to move the hoops.

Step 4 – Install the Purlins
Although the hoops are in place, they are not currently strong enough to keep the hoop house up. You now need to install the purlins, which are the horizontal pipes linking the hoops together adding stability and strength.

You need at least one (some people will install two – one just on either side of the peak) along the ridge of your polytunnel. Two more are needed part way down each side.

If you live in a region with particularly strong winds, then you may want to consider adding extra purlins for more strength.

The purlin pipes are positioned on the inside of the hoops. Use ¼" carriage bolts to secure them together, making sure the bolt will not damage the plastic sheeting.

If you have decided to make roll-up sides, then you will need to build a wooden framework wherever you are planning to have this ventilation. The roll-up plastic will hang from this frame.

Step 5 – Adding the Plastic

Protective tape needs to be applied to all parts of the frame that are going to touch the plastic. There can be a chemical reaction between the PVC pipes and the polyethylene plastic sheeting which will cause the plastic sheeting to age more rapidly than normal, becoming brittle. The tape also prevents bolt heads from causing any damage to the sheeting.

This is best done on a calm day as it can be extremely difficult to put the plastic in place if there is any wind.

You need to choose the best grade plastic you can find. A 6mm UV protected greenhouse plastic will last a good four or five years plus provide good insulation. Cheaper plastics have a tendency to degrade more rapidly in sunlight meaning you need to replace it every year or two.

Unroll the plastic ready to cover your hoop house, leaving at least a foot of extra plastic along the long sides. At each end leave two feet of extra plastic.

The easy way to put the plastic in place can be done with just two of you though the more people you have to help pull the plastic in place the better.

Wrap the excess plastic around some small sponge balls (about the size of tennis balls) every 5 feet along one long side of the sheeting. Tie the balls in place using some rope.

Throw the other end of the ropes over the peak of your hoop house and then carefully pull the plastic in place. It can be helpful to have some stepladders to hand to reduce the strain on the framework and in case of any difficulties.

Now make sure the plastic is aligned and straight on the frame. Your plastic may have fold marks in it which are useful as visual markers.

The best way to secure the plastic to the wooden ground frame is to use something called wiggle wire. This fastens into an aluminum track which is fastened to this wooden frame. It's a very good way of securing your sheeting securely.

An alternative is to wrap the extra plastic around some 1x2" wood and then secure it to the ground frame.

If you live in a particularly windy area, then you can use duckbill anchors to secure the ground frame. One needs to go in each corner and then another couple along each long side.

One thing you can do is create a double layer of plastic on your hoop house. The second layer of plastic is pulled over your frame and secured leaving some slack. Small electric fans are then used to blow air between the two layers of plastic, inflating them away from each other. This provides better insulation and helps to prevent the plastic flapping in the wind.

Make sure that the plastic sheeting is tight because you do not want water to pool on the roof. The extra weight could damage your hoop house. During particularly heavy rain you may want to visit your hoop house to make sure no water is pooling on the roof.

Step 6 – Building the End Walls

The end walls are best made from either 2x3" or 2x4" timber. A wooden framework is built and attached to the piping. You can either use wiggle wire to secure the plastic, or you can use wooden batons.

Remember that at one end you will need a door which can be as simple as a flap or can be a wooden framework on hinges.

The Flooring

Although you can leave the floor open to the soil, I wouldn't recommend it. If you do, then all you have done is built a nice warm environment for weeds to grow in. You will be spending a lot of time tackling weeds plus you run the risk of damaging your plastic sheeting while digging the soil.

You can pave the floor or concrete it if you want to go to that expense and effort. A lot of people though will use a very high-quality weed membrane, often in a double layer, to suppress weeds and provide a surface for your plants to grow in containers.

You can see in the picture what happens if you do not put down a proper floor. The wood on either side of that picture is staging which stands just over 3' tall! The weeds have taken over this tunnel and are loving the protective environment.

I wouldn't recommend putting down bark because it will need replacing every couple of years and will break down, allowing weeds to grow. It is a nightmare to replace, and you have to find something to do with all the rotten bark!

If you don't want to build your own polytunnel then you can buy them cheaply enough. Remember though to buy one that using strong pipes and plastic sheeting. If these are too weak, then they are going to be damaged in high winds or heavy rain.

Your hoop house, once built, can be used pretty much like a greenhouse. The same principles of cleanliness and management apply. Depending on where you live you may want to remove the plastic sheeting during the winter months to prevent damage, but you can leave it on and overwinter plants in your polytunnel.

MAKING MONEY WITH YOUR GREENHOUSE

A greenhouse is a great addition to any garden, but you can use your glass house to turn a profit. If you are growing on an allotment, you need to check the site rules as some do not permit you to sell anything grown on your plot. If you are growing in your garden, you should check local laws to see if there are any regulations that apply to you.

Even with a small greenhouse, there are still ways for you to turn a profit without making too much extra work for yourself.

Firstly, let's look at some of the most profitable crops you can grow in a greenhouse. These are very cash rich crops that are quite easy to grow and can be sold on to suppliers, health food shops, and local companies.

Ginseng
This is a very popular healing herb that commands a high price. It isn't a quick crop to mature though and can take up to six years for the roots to mature enough to be harvested.

Gourmet Mushrooms
High-end mushrooms such as oyster and shitake are very popular, and expensive, mushrooms. These are popular with restaurants and on farmer markets, commanding a good price. A square foot of space can produce around 25lbs or mushrooms per year. When you are selling directly to consumers such as through Farmer's markets or to restaurants you can get at least $7 per pound of mushrooms.

Bamboo
This is a very fast growing plant, known to grow more than two feet in a single day! It is extremely popular as a landscaping plant and is in high demand by gardeners across the country. They are best grown in containers and will thrive even in cold weather. Larger containers can sell for a couple of hundred dollars per plant though smaller plants can easily be sold at local markets or to a local garden store. Decorative varieties are particularly popular with buyers.

Cacti
These can be very collectable, particularly the rarer varieties. They can grow very well in your greenhouse and don't tend to mind the cold weather. Many thrive on neglect and can be put into nice pots and sold at farmers

markets or similar events.

Herbs

Herbs are another profitable crop as many restaurants, and home chefs like to use fresh herbs. You may even be able to sell them into local grocery stores too or at Farmer's markets. Of course as well as fresh herbs you could dry the herbs and sell them yourself. Popular herbs include basil, cilantro, chives, oregano, and parsley. The plants are sold at a size where they are ready to harvest.

Chilies

These are a very popular plant to grow and can be extremely popular when sold fresh, dried or powdered.

Many people love their chilies but getting their hands on any of the hotter and more unusual varieties is almost impossible. Growing these different chili plants as well as very hot chilies can be very profitable when sold to the consumer market through the Internet or Farmer's markets. Some local stores and restaurants will take them too.

Medical Marijuana

This is an extremely profitable crop but it is not legal everywhere and where it is legal growers often need to be licensed. It is a controversial choice, but if you are looking for a profitable crop and it is legal in your area, then this is an extremely good way to create an income from your greenhouse. Just make sure you follow your local laws to the letter as you don't want to get into any trouble!

Other Money Making Ideas

Whether you decide to grow seedlings to sell or wait until you have a harvest, there are many potential markets for your crops and many potential profitable crops. A lot of it will depend on what is available in your area and what sells. It may be worth taking some time to visit some of these potential markets and find out what is selling and at what price. You can then decide whether or not it is profitable for you to enter that market.

Flea Markets

These are a great market for excess plants and typically run throughout the year. You pay a fixed price to sell at the flea market, and then you keep any profit that you make. It is a good way to sell your plants, particularly if you have grown unusual varieties of popular crops, e.g. black tomatoes, yellow zucchini, chilies and so on.

Florists

Local florists (rather than national chains) may well take your excess plants on a sale or return basis. They could also take cut or potted flowers too. It is worth talking to the florist and asking them what they would buy to determine how profitable it would be. If you are selling flowers to them, then they will want high quality, perfect flowers.

Farmer's Markets

These are very similar to flea markets but tend to focus purely on fruits, vegetables, plants and sometimes flowers. Again you pay for space and then keep any money you make, but you may find a regular seller who will share their space or split the cost with a fellow gardener. Make sure you know what prices you can get for your produce to understand if it is worth your while.

Health Food Stores

These can be a good market for fresh or dried herbs, plants with healing properties and even sometimes fresh vegetables. Most local health food shops (not so much with national chains) are keen to work with local suppliers. If you can provide fresh potted herbs out of season, then these can command a premium price.

Pet Stores

You may be wondering what you could sell to pet stores, but potted catnip or cat grass for cats sells very well. Hamsters and birds like certain types of grasses. Selling these in 3" or 4" pots to your local pet store can be a great earner, particularly as they know they are getting fresh, healthy plants. If you can provide a constant supply, then you can win against national suppliers who deliver once or twice a month.

The Internet

Online is the obvious place to sell your produce, including seeds from desirable plants. However, you need to be aware of state laws as not everything can be shipped between states and countries. If you are selling live plants, then you need to factor in the cost of safely packaging and posting them into your profitability calculations. Often the cost of shipping can be prohibitive as you have to use courier companies to deliver live plants.

Selling Seeds

Most gardeners are thoroughly addicted to buying seeds, particularly for unusual varieties of plant. Heirloom seeds of any kind are extremely popular and worth looking into. You can let some of your plants go to seed and then sell the dried seeds. Of course, look at state/country regulations as you may be limited where you can ship, but it can be a good earner for you.

These are just some of the potential markets open to you for making money from your greenhouse. Of course, not everyone will want to turn their hobby into a business. You can still use your greenhouse just for growing stuff for yourself, but if you are looking for some extra income, then a greenhouse can certainly be used to turn a profit.

There are plenty of potential markets, but ultimately you need to do some legwork and find out what the potential markets are in your area. You can even tap into seasonal events, e.g. selling Christmas plants at Christmas or cut/potted flowers at Mother's Day.

There are lots and lots of ideas, and with a greenhouse, you may find it easier to turn your hobby into a profitable business venture.

ENDNOTE

A greenhouse is a must have for any gardener. It has so many potential uses and makes your life so much easier that you will wonder how you ever managed without one.

You can spend as much, or as little, money as you want on your greenhouse, it depends on your budget. However, what is important is that you choose the site and then prepare it properly. Doing so will reduce the amount of maintenance you need to do and extend the lifespan of your greenhouse.

Your greenhouse needs to be secure against the wind and any potential damage from the surroundings, think footballs and falling branches. Set up properly it will be very low maintenance and an absolutely pleasure to grow in.

You will be able to extend your growing season, being able to start your seeds off earlier in the year and grow delicate crops longer into the cooler months. For anyone outside of the warmest areas, it is essential as it will make the difference when it comes to getting your crops to produce a viable harvest.

This book has tried to answer all of your potential questions and show you the many benefits of a greenhouse. With everything you have learned in this book, you will now be able to set up your greenhouse and manage it easily. It will reduce the amount of work you need to do and allow you to grow plants that would otherwise have been out of your reach.

You do have to remember that greenhouses come with their own potential set of problems. However, most of these can be avoided purely by ensuring there is suitable ventilation and air circulation. These two issues are by far the number one cause of problems within any glass house.

Pollination can be an issue but leaving vents open will allow pollinating insects in and, as you learnt earlier, you can always pollinate your plants by hand.

It is vital that you either have a suitable irrigation system in your greenhouse or that you water your plants regularly. On hotter days they will require daily watering, particularly if they are in smaller containers. Lack of water causes leaf, flower and fruit drop which will impact your potential harvest.

If you are planning on putting a greenhouse in your garden or on your allotment, then I'd recommend you go and size it up. Look for a suitable space and measure it up to determine what size greenhouse you can put in.

You may decide to start with a portable greenhouse or a hoop house, depending on the space and budget available to you.

Making the decisions about the type of floor and foundation need to be made right at the start as these are very difficult, and expensive, to change later on. I wouldn't recommend growing directly in the soil as it will quickly become a burden and turn your greenhouse into a chore.

I will guarantee that in your first year you will overcrowd your greenhouse in your excitement. By the second you will want another greenhouse or a bigger one as you understand the benefits and how great a greenhouse is. I'm currently looking at putting a second greenhouse on my plot and a 25-foot long poly tunnel (hoop house). I can see so many benefits, and after a couple of poor growing years, this will make a massive difference to my ability to produce the more delicate crops I like.

Owning a greenhouse is a lot of fun and full of potential. I would highly recommend you get one, as large as you can afford and fit in. You will enjoy it immensely as it allows you to successful grow a wide variety of crops that you would otherwise have struggled to grow. These useful glass houses are well worth the investment and will give you years of enjoyment and growing pleasure.

ABOUT JASON

Jason has been a keen gardener for over twenty years, having taken on numerous weed infested patches and turned them into productive vegetable gardens.

One of his first gardening experiences was digging over a 400 square foot garden in its entirety and turning it into a vegetable garden, much to the delight of his neighbors who all got free vegetables! It was through this experience that he discovered his love of gardening and started to learn more about the subject.

His first encounter with a greenhouse resulted in a tomato infested greenhouse but he soon learnt how to make the most of a greenhouse and now grows a wide variety of plants from grapes to squashes to tomatoes and more. Of course, his wife is delighted with his greenhouse as it means the windowsills in the house are no longer filled with seed trays every spring.

He is passionate about helping people learn to grow their own fresh produce and enjoy the many benefits that come with it, from the exercise of gardening to the nutrition of freshly picked produce. He often says that when you've tasted a freshly picked tomato you'll never want to buy another one from a store again!

Jason is also very active in the personal development community, having written books on self-help, including subjects such as motivation and confidence. He has also recorded over 80 hypnosis programs, being a fully qualified clinical hypnotist which he sells from his website www.MusicForChange.com.

He hopes that this book has been a pleasure for you to read and that you have learned a lot about the subject and welcomes your feedback either directly or through an Amazon review. This feedback is used to improve his books and provide better quality information for his readers.

Jason also loves to grow giant and unusual vegetables and is still planning on breaking the 400lb barrier with a giant pumpkin. He hopes that with his new allotment plot he'll be able to grow even more exciting vegetables to share with his readers.

OTHER BOOKS BY JASON

Please check out my other gardening books on Amazon, available in Kindle and paperback.

Berry Gardening – The Complete Guide to Berry Gardening from Gooseberries to Boysenberries and More

Who doesn't love fresh berries? Find out how you can grow many of the popular berries at home such as marion berries and blackberries and some of the more unusual like honeyberries and goji berries. A step by step guide to growing your own berries including pruning, propagating and more. Discover how you can grow a wide variety of berries at home in your garden or on your balcony.

Canning and Preserving at Home – A Complete Guide to Canning, Preserving and Storing Your Produce

A complete guide to storing your home-grown fruits and vegetables. Learn everything from how to freeze your produce to canning, making jams, jellies, and chutneys to dehydrating and more. Everything you need to know about storing your fresh produce, including some unusual methods of storage, some of which will encourage children to eat fresh fruit!

Companion Planting Secrets – Organic Gardening to Deter Pests and Increase Yield

Learn the secrets of natural and organic pest control with companion planting. This is a great way to increase your yield, produce better quality plants and work in harmony with nature. By attracting beneficial insects to your garden, you can naturally keep down harmful pests and reduce the damage they cause. You probably grow many of these companion plants already, but by repositioning them, you can reap the many benefits of this natural method of gardening.

Container Gardening - Growing Vegetables, Herbs & Flowers in Containers

A step by step guide showing you how to create your very own container garden. Whether you have no garden, little space or you want to grow specific plants, this book guides you through everything you need to know about planting a container garden from the different types of pots, to which plants thrive in containers to handy tips helping you avoid the common mistakes people make with containers.

Cooking with Zucchini - Delicious Recipes, Preserves and More With Courgettes: How To Deal With A Glut Of Zucchini And Love It!

Getting too many zucchinis from your plants? This book teaches you how to grow your own courgettes at home as well as showing you the many different varieties you could grow. Packed full of delicious recipes, you will learn everything from the famous zucchini chocolate cake to delicious main courses, snacks, and Paleo diet friendly raw recipes. The must have guide for anyone dealing with a glut of zucchini.

Environmentally Friendly Gardening - - Your Guide to a Sustainable Eco-Friendly Garden

A guide to making your garden more environmentally friendly, from looking after beneficial insects and wildlife, to saving water and reducing plastic use. There is a lot you can do to reduce your reliance on chemicals and work in harmony with nature, while still having a beautiful and productive garden. This book details many things you can easily do to become more eco-friendly in your garden.

Growing Brassicas – Growing Cruciferous Vegetables from Broccoli to Mooli to Wasabi and More

Brassicas are renowned for their health benefits and are packed full of vitamins. They are easy to grow at home, but beset by problems. Find out how you can grow these amazing vegetables at home, including the incredibly beneficial plants broccoli and maca. Includes step by step growing guides plus delicious recipes for every recipe!

Growing Chilies – A Beginners Guide to Growing, Using & Surviving Chilies

Ever wanted to grow super-hot chilies? Or maybe you just want to grow your own chilies to add some flavor to your food? This book is your complete, step-by-step guide to growing chilies at home. With topics from selecting varieties to how to germinate seeds, you will learn everything you need to know to grow chilies successfully, even the notoriously difficult to grow varieties such as Carolina Reaper. With recipes for sauces, meals and making your own chili powder, you'll find everything you need to know to grow your own chili plants

Growing Fruit: The Complete Guide to Growing Fruit at Home

This is a complete guide to growing fruit from apricots to walnuts and everything in between. You will learn how to choose fruit plants, how to grow and care for them, how to store and preserve the fruit and much more. With recipes, advice, and tips this is the perfect book for anyone who wants to learn more about growing fruit at home, whether beginner or experienced gardener.

Growing Garlic – A Complete Guide to Growing, Harvesting & Using Garlic

Everything you need to know to grow this popular plant. Whether you are growing normal garlic or elephant garlic for cooking or health, you will find this book contains all the information you need. Traditionally a difficult crop to grow with a long growing season, you'll learn the exact conditions garlic needs, how to avoid the common problems people encounter and how to store your garlic for use all year round. A complete, step-by-step guide showing you precisely how to grow garlic at home.

Growing Herbs – A Beginners Guide To Growing, Using, Harvesting and Storing Herbs

A comprehensive guide to growing herbs at home, detailing 49 different herbs. Learn everything you need to know to grow these herbs from their preferred soil conditions to how to harvest and propagate them and more. Including recipes for health and beauty plus delicious dishes to make in your kitchen. This step-by-step guide is designed to teach you all about growing herbs at home, from a few herbs in containers to a fully-fledged herb garden. An indispensable guide to growing and using herbs.

Growing Giant Pumpkins – How to Grow Massive Pumpkins at Home

A complete step by step guide detailing everything you need to know to produce pumpkins weighing hundreds of pounds, if not edging into the thousands! Anyone can grow giant pumpkins at home, and this book gives you the insider secrets of the giant pumpkin growers showing you how to avoid the mistakes people commonly make when trying to grow a giant pumpkin. This is a complete guide detailing everything from preparing the soil to getting the right seeds to germinating the seeds and caring for your pumpkins.

Growing Lavender: Growing, Using, Cooking and Healing with Lavender

A complete guide to growing and using this beautiful plant. Find out about the hundreds of different varieties of lavender and how you can grow this bee friendly plant at home. With hundreds of uses in crafts, cooking and healing, this plant has a long history of association with humans. Discover today how you can grow lavender at home and enjoy this amazing herb.

Growing Tomatoes: Your Guide to Growing Delicious Tomatoes at Home

This is the definitive guide to growing delicious and fresh tomatoes at home. Teaching you everything from selecting seeds to planting and caring for your tomatoes as well as diagnosing problems this is the ideal book for anyone who wants to grow tomatoes at home. A comprehensive must have guide.

How to Compost – Turn Your Waste into Brown Gold

This is a complete step by step guide to making your own compost at home. Vital to any gardener, this book will explain everything from setting up your compost heap to how to ensure you get fresh compost in just a few weeks. A must have handbook for any gardener who wants their plants to benefit from home-made compost.

How to Grow Potatoes - The Guide To Choosing, Planting and Growing in Containers Or the Ground

Learn everything you need to know about growing potatoes at home. Discover the wide variety of potatoes you can grow, many delicious varieties you will never see in the shops. Find out the best way to grow potatoes at home, how to protect your plants from the many pests and diseases and how to store your harvest so you can enjoy fresh potatoes over winter. A complete step by step guide telling you everything you need to know to grow potatoes at home successfully.

Hydroponics: A Beginners Guide to Growing Food without Soil

Hydroponics is growing plants without soil, which is a fantastic idea for indoor gardens. It is surprisingly easy to set up, once you know what you are doing and is significantly more productive and quicker than growing in soil. This book will tell you everything you need to know to get started growing flowers, vegetables and fruit hydroponically at home.

Indoor Gardening for Beginners: The Complete Guide to Growing Herbs, Flowers, Vegetables and Fruits in Your House

Discover how you can grow a wide variety of plants in your home. Whether you want to grow herbs for cooking, vegetables or a decorative plant display, this book tells you everything you need to know. Learn which plants to keep in your home to purify the air and remove harmful chemicals and how to successfully grow plants from cacti to flowers to carnivorous plants.

Keeping Chickens for Beginners – Keeping Backyard Chickens from Coops to Feeding to Care and More

Chickens are becoming very popular to keep at home, but it isn't something you should leap into without the right information. This book guides you through everything you need to know to keep chickens from decided what breed to what coop to how to feed them, look after them and keep your chickens healthy and producing eggs. This is your complete guide to owning chickens, with absolutely everything you need to know to get started and successfully keep chickens at home.

Raised Bed Gardening – A Guide to Growing Vegetables In Raised Beds

Learn why raised beds are such an efficient and effortless way to garden as you discover the benefits of no-dig gardening, denser planting and less bending, ideal for anyone who hates weeding or suffers from back pain.

You will learn everything you need to know to build your own raised beds, plant them and ensure they are highly productive.

Vertical Gardening: Maximum Productivity, Minimum Space

This is an exciting form of gardening allows you to grow large amounts of fruit and vegetables in small areas, maximizing your use of space. Whether you have a large garden, an allotment or just a small balcony, you will be able to grow more delicious fresh produce. Find out how I grew over 70 strawberry plants in just three feet of ground space and more in this detailed guide.

Worm Farming: Creating Compost at Home with Vermiculture

Learn about this amazing way of producing high-quality compost at home by recycling your kitchen waste. Worms break it down and produce a sought after, highly nutritious compost that your plants will thrive in. No matter how big your garden you will be able to create your own worm farm and compost using the techniques in this step-by-step guide. Learn how to start worm farming and producing your own high-quality compost at home.

WANT MORE INSPIRING GARDENING IDEAS?

This book is part of the Inspiring Gardening Ideas series. Bringing you the best books anywhere on how to get the most from your garden or allotment.

You can find out about more wonderful books just like this one at: www.OwningAnAllotment.com

Follow me at www.YouTube.com/OwningAnAllotment for my video diary and tips. Join me on Facebook for regular updates and discussions at www.Facebook.com/OwningAnAllotment.

Find me on Instagram and Twitter as @allotmentowner where I post regular updates, offers and gardening news. Follow me today and let's catch up in person!

Thank you for reading!

CPSIA information can be obtained
at www.ICGtesting.com
Printed in the USA
BVHW011104210221
600725BV00015B/535

9 781838 336004